# THE DESIGN OF
# BUSINESS

# THE DESIGN OF
# BUSINESS

*Why Design Thinking Is
the Next Competitive Advantage*

## Roger Martin

HARVARD BUSINESS PRESS

BOSTON, MASSACHUSETTS

Library of Congress Cataloging-in-Publication Data
Martin, Roger L.
    The design of business: why design thinking is the next competitive advantage / Roger Martin.
        p. cm.
    ISBN 978-1-4221-7780-8 (hbk. : alk. paper)
  1.   Creative ability in business.  2.   Lateral thinking.  3.   Creative thinking.
4.   Knowledge management.  5.   Management.  I.   Title.
    HD53.M3644 2009
    650.4'063—dc22

                                                            2009021389

*Dedicated to Jennifer*

# Contents

# Acknowledgments

I have many generous friends and colleagues to thank for their help on this book. In particular, I would like to thank and recognize three intellectual partners: Hilary Austen, Mihnea Moldoveanu, and Jennifer Riel.

Hilary Austen has had a profound influence on the way I think about design. The model for building one's personal design capability, which is outlined in chapter 7, is based directly on Hilary's work on artistry. I am thrilled that she is (finally) capturing her brilliant work in a book, tentatively titled *Artistry: How to Achieve and Enjoy Great Performance.* I believe that it has a chance to be the best book on artistry since John Dewey's 1934 masterpiece, *Art as Experience.*

Mihnea Moldoveanu, director of the Desautels Centre for Integrative Thinking, has been my closest and most important thinking partner since he joined me at the Rotman School a decade ago. We collaborate on numerous projects, and very little that I write cannot be traced back to one of our many conversations. You will see his insightful sidebars at various points in the book. I am particularly indebted to Mihnea for introducing me to the wonderful work of Charles Sanders Peirce, who is sufficiently obscure that only a polymath like Mihnea would have discovered his potential contribution to our work.

Jennifer Riel, who is associate director of the Desautels Centre, played the primary editing and research role on this book. She became ever more centrally involved in its evolution over the past year. Her advice was enormously helpful, her editing shaped and improved the book, and her discipline ensured that the manuscript met every deadline. You will see Jennifer's nicely crafted sidebars at various points.

I would also like to thank three people who let me interview them extensively. Claudia Kotchka, a dear friend and Procter & Gamble's first vice president of innovation strategy and design, gave me lots of time and insights and also provided detailed feedback on the first manuscript of the book. Mike Lazaridis, founder of Research In Motion, creator of the ubiquitous BlackBerry, and one of the busiest people I have ever met, was very generous with his time and thoughts. Dr. Stephen Scherer, a world-renowned geneticist at the Hospital for Sick Children, not only let me interview him but gave me an extensive tour of his laboratory. What an eye-opener that was!

The primary financial supporter of my work in integrative thinking and design is my wise and far-thinking friend Marcel Desautels. Without his support and devotion, DesignWorks would have been one project, not a vibrant research and action-learning center. I would also like to thank Heather Fraser, the terrific leader I hired to head Rotman DesignWorks. She has done a wonderful job of building DesignWorks and furthering both the intellectual development and the practical application of the concepts in this book.

My designer friends were helpful and generous. Tim Brown and David Kelley of IDEO and Sohrab Voussoughi of Ziba

answered a series of questions for me; their insights are dotted throughout. Bill Buxton of Microsoft and John Maeda, president of Rhode Island School of Design, did likewise and in addition reviewed the draft manuscript for me.

Deep in my past, three people strongly influenced my interest in design in business, and I probably would not have written this book without them. The husband and wife team of Bob Hambly and Barb Woolley (of the design firm Hambly & Woolley) have been my friends for twenty-five years and first got me interested in design. They played an important role by inviting me to be a keynote speaker for a 2003 design conference, which created an excuse to organize my thinking on design into a talk I called "The Design of Business." It went over so well at the conference that I was motivated to write an article by the same name based on the conference presentation. Shockingly to me, publications from over a dozen countries saw the article in *Rotman Magazine* and asked permission to republish it in their country (and language). The high demand for the article encouraged me to write the book. So without Bob and Barb, I am not sure this book would have happened. By the way, Bob and Barb designed a number of the figures in this book, including "The Knowledge Funnel." The third important influence is Rob Harvey, whom I met in 1993 when he was the senior vice president of design at Herman Miller. He was so passionate about design that he made it impossible for me to ever think again in the traditional ways I had thought about business.

I am fortunate to have a wonderful group of friends who reviewed the draft manuscript and gave helpful comments. First and foremost was Malcolm Gladwell, whose three-thousand-word critique was a thing of beauty and dramatically altered the structure of the book—for the better to be sure. In addition to those already mentioned, I received helpful reviews from Brendan Calder, Melanie Carr, Delaine Hampton, Bruce Kuwabara, A. G. Lafley, Sally Osberg, Filippo Passerini, Joe Rotman, Suzanne Spragge, Patrick Whitney, and Craig Wynett.

Jennifer Riel and I also got valuable research help from Sean Forbes, Signy Franklin, Albert Ko, and Mark Leung.

I got fabulous help and support for my writing at the Rotman School. Karen Christensen, who publishes our wonderful *Rotman Magazine*, jumped on the design theme early and encouraged me to write several design articles for the magazine, pieces of which found their way into the book. Steve Arenburg and Ken McGuffin in media relations and events provided opportunities for me to write about design in business in publications such as *Fast Company* and *BusinessWeek* and speak at conferences in New York, San Francisco, Hong Kong, and London. Each time I wrote or spoke about design, I got feedback that helped me refine my thinking. And when I took off the summers of 2007 and 2008 to write, my great vice deans Jim Fisher and Peter Pauly and stellar chief operating officer Mary-Ellen Yeomans ran the school so efficiently that no one noticed I was gone!

This is my second book with Jeff Kehoe and his terrific team at Harvard Business Press. It was wonderful to work with Jeff a second time. I appreciated both his advice and his support through the book's long gestation. It is my second collaboration with editor Harris Collingwood, who also worked on *The Opposable Mind*. Harris was a delight to work with—a consummate writing professional whose instinct to shorten and simplify everything I write is well placed.

Last, but certainly not least, I want to thank the incomparable Tina Bennett—*uber* agent. I owe my book publishing career (such as it is) to this talented woman. She helps shape each project to make it exciting for the publishers and makes everything move like clockwork. I look forward to many more collaborations with Tina.

I do hope you enjoy this book and that it helps you express your personal and organizational creativity to the fullest. If I have contributed even in a small way to that optimization, I will be a happy author!

# 1

# The Knowledge Funnel

*How Discovery Takes Shape*

THE UNITED STATES in the years after World War II was a restless place, engaged in an audacious social experiment that would eventually transform how and where Americans worked, played, and consumed. Victorious with the Allied nations against the Axis, then instrumental in the rebuilding of Europe, the United States had become the West's undisputed military and economic champion. Not all was cheery, mind you. Communist powers posed a new threat, the nuclear age had dawned, and Cold War anxieties ran high. Yet Americans felt confident in their place atop the global order and free to invent new ways to enjoy their burgeoning prosperity.

The automobile was central to the sense of open-ended possibility shared by America's rapidly growing middle class. Spurred by the development of the Interstate Highway System, new roads were rolling out from the cities to the suburbs springing up at their edges. The number of cars sold in America leapt from just seventy thousand in 1945 to more than six million in 1950. A mobile, moneyed lifestyle was taking root, with the automobile at its center.

Some of the first entrepreneurs to see the opportunities in this cultural change planted their flags in California, where so many American trends first take root. Drive-in burger joints began to spring up across southern California, where the nascent car culture cross-fertilized a leisure culture centered on the beach. By 1955, a strong-willed salesman named Ray Kroc was able to make a good living selling milk-shake mixers to a wide collection of mom-and-pop California restaurants. His biggest account was the McDonald brothers, who operated a small but thriving chain of drive-ins in the Los Angeles suburbs.[1]

The brothers had opened their first restaurant, a barbeque and burger drive-in in San Bernardino, in 1940. It wasn't much different from other drive-ins, which had been popping up ever since A&W first delivered root beer to car windows in 1923. But it was popular. The McDonald's outpost attracted throngs of teenagers, with harried carhops serving up to a hundred twenty-five carloads at a time.

Within the decade, though, the McDonald brothers realized they had to revamp their restaurant or find a new line of work. Some of their best customers were families giving mom a night off from the kitchen. But now these families were driving right past, turned off by the loitering toughs that drive-ins attracted. Many of the remaining customers complained that the food got cold on the journey from kitchen to car. The McDonald brothers needed a new approach, but what? How and what did Californians want to eat when they set out in their Fords and Buicks and Studebakers in determined pursuit of sun and surf?

The brothers experimented with different menus and store formats until they arrived at a winning approach. They filled in the barbeque pit, cut the menu to only twenty-five items, and standardized the burgers; each one was served with ketchup, mustard, onions, and two pickle slices. The carhops were eliminated, replaced with service windows where customers ordered and picked up their own food. Productivity enhancers like Kroc's five-at-a-time milk-shake mixers enabled them to turn food orders around quickly. The brothers called their new concept the Speedee Service System. It was the prototype of the quick-service restaurant.

It wasn't long before the brothers had opened four additional outlets. They might have been content to stop there, but Kroc was not. He looked at the crowds packed into the brothers' stores and imagined the scene repeated from coast to coast—and even around the world. He bought out the McDonalds and set about improving and standardizing the mass-production system they had developed.

Kroc saw that the Speedee Service System, innovative as it was, left too much to chance and judgment. He refined it meticulously, pursuing a vision of a perfectly standardized operation. He simplified the McDonald's system down to an exact science, with a rigid set of rules that spelled out *exactly* how long to cook a hamburger, *exactly* how to hire people, *exactly* how to choose locations, *exactly* how to manage stores, and *exactly* how to franchise them. Under Kroc, nothing in the McDonald's kitchen was left to chance: every hamburger came out of a stamping machine weighing exactly 1.6 ounces, its thickness measured to the thousandth of an inch, and the cooking process stopped automatically after 38 seconds, when the burgers reached an internal temperature of exactly 155 degrees. In every phase of McDonald's operations, judgment was removed, possibilities were removed, and variety was removed.

Kroc relentlessly stripped away uncertainty, ambiguity, and judgment from the processes that emerged from the McDonald brothers' original insight. And by fine-tuning the formula, he powered McDonald's from a modestly prosperous chain of burger restaurants to a scale previously undreamed of. Within a decade, McDonald's grew from a successful local business to a ubiquitous cross-country chain and, in another few decades, to a globe-girdling behemoth.

The path taken by the McDonald's and Kroc—from pinpointing a market opportunity to devising an offering for that market to codifying its operations—is not just a study in entrepreneurship. It's a model for how businesses of all sorts can advance knowledge and capture value. I will argue in this book that the McDonald brothers and Kroc took the same route followed by successful business innovators in every domain. My term for that path is the *knowledge funnel*. My purpose is to map that funnel in detail and investigate its implications for organizations, individuals, and thinking processes. Along the way, we'll meet innovators in business, science, and the arts, all of whom are advancing understanding and creating exciting new opportunities for people and organizations.

## Seeking Reconciliation

The model for value creation offered in this book requires a balance—or more accurately a reconciliation—between two prevailing points of view on business today. One school of thought, put forward by some of the world's most respected theorists and consultants, holds that the path to value creation lies in driving out the old-fashioned practice of gut feelings and instincts, replacing it with strategy based on rigorous, quantitative analysis (optimally backed by decision-support software). In this model, the basis of thought is *analytical thinking*, which harnesses two familiar forms of logic—deductive reasoning and inductive reasoning—to declare truths and certainties about the world. The goal of this model is mastery through rigorous, continuously repeated analytical processes. Judgment, bias, and variation are the enemies. If they are vanquished, the theory goes, great decisions will be made and great value will be created.

The opposing school of thought, which is in many ways a reaction to the rise of analytical management, is centered on the primacy of creativity and innovation. To this school, analysis has driven out creativity and doomed organizations to boring stultification. "The minute you start analyzing and using consumer research, you drive all the creativity out of the product," the vice chairman and chief of design for a world-leading American firm told me recently. "No good product was ever created from quantitative market research. Great products spring from the heart and soul of a great designer, unencumbered by committees, processes, or analyses." To proponents of this philosophy, the creative instinct—the unanalyzed flash of insight—is venerated as the source of true innovation. At the heart of this school is *intuitive thinking*—the art of knowing without reasoning. This is the world of originality and invention.

These two models seem utterly incommensurable; an organization must choose to embrace either analysis or intuition as the primary driver of value creation. This choice then plays out in the structure and norms of the organization. Organizations dominated by analytical thinking are built to operate as they always have; they are structurally resistant to the idea of designing and redesigning themselves and their business dynamically over time. They are built to maintain the status quo. By sticking closely to the tried and true, organizations dominated by analytical thinking enjoy one very important advantage: they can build size and scale. In organizations dominated by intuitive thinking, on the other hand, innovation may come fast and furiously, but growth and longevity represent tremendous challenges. Intuition-biased firms cannot and will not systematize what they do, so they wax and wane with individual intuitive leaders.

Neither analysis nor intuition alone is enough. Rather than forcing a binary choice to drive out either analysis or intuition, the burden of this book is to reconcile the two modes of thought. I will argue that aspects of both analytical and intuitive thinking are necessary but not sufficient for optimal business performance. The most successful businesses in the years to come will balance analytical mastery and intuitive originality in a dynamic interplay that I call *design thinking*. Design thinking is the form of thought that enables movement along the knowledge funnel, and the firms that master it will gain a nearly inexhaustible, long-term business advantage. The advantage, which emerges from the design-thinking firms' unwavering focus on the creative design of systems, will eventually extend to the wider world. From these firms will emerge the breakthroughs that move the world forward.

Design-thinking firms stand apart in their willingness to engage in the task of continuously redesigning their business. They do so with an eye to creating advances in both innovation and efficiency—the combination that produces the most powerful competitive edge. This is not to suggest that only design-thinking firms pursue innovation. No, the value that business leaders place on innovation is reflected in the wealth of resources that they devote to its pursuit. But in all too many cases, businesses unwittingly work against their own purposes. Even as corporate leaders chase the vital, elusive spark of creativity, their organizations' structures, processes, and norms extinguish it wherever it flares up. Their cultures and routines privilege analysis over intuition and mastery over originality.

As A. G. Lafley has demonstrated at Procter & Gamble, however, even organizations with a deeply ingrained bias toward analysis and mastery can develop powerful capacities for innovation. With determined leadership, they can develop the skills, structures, and processes that generate value by driving valuable insights along the knowledge funnel. Figure 1-1 shows how knowledge proceeds through the funnel.

The first stage of the funnel is the exploration of a *mystery*, which takes an infinite variety of forms. A research scientist might explore the mystery of a syndrome such as autism. A hospital administrator might ask what kind of space would improve the condition of cancer patients coping with chemotherapy. Or an

**FIGURE 1-1**

## The knowledge funnel

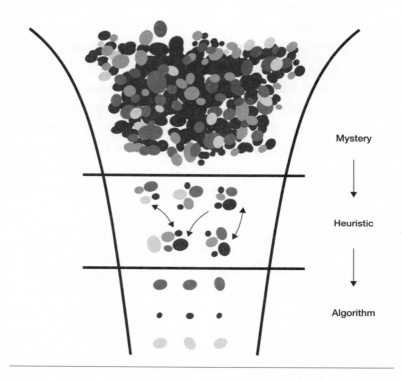

Mystery

Heuristic

Algorithm

ambitious salesman might ask how and what Americans would like to eat on the go.

The next stage of the funnel is a *heuristic*, a rule of thumb that helps narrow the field of inquiry and work the mystery down to a manageable size. The heuristic may be a genetic anomaly, a user-centered approach to the process flow of a chemotherapy patient, or the concept of a quick-service, drive-through restaurant. It is a way of thinking about the mystery that provides a simplified understanding of it and allows those with access to the heuristic to focus their efforts.

As an organization puts its heuristic into operation, studies it more, and thinks about it intensely, it can convert from a general rule of thumb (Americans want a quick, convenient, tasty meal) to a fixed formula (Kroc's totally systematized McDonald's). That formula is an *algorithm*, the last of three stages of the knowledge funnel. (For another perspective on the path through the knowledge funnel, see "Hunches, Heuristics, and Algorithmics: A Quick Note.")

Each stage of the knowledge funnel has its own unique features that are worth examining in some detail. It is said that the road to wisdom begins with ignorance, and that is where we begin.

## It Starts with a Question

Over the course of time, phenomena enter our collective consciousness as mysteries—things in our environment that excite our curiosity but elude our understanding. The mystery of what we now know as gravity confounded our ancestors: when they looked around them, they saw that most objects—apples, famously— seemed to fall to the ground quickly; but others, such as leaves, seemed to take forever to reach the ground. And then there were birds, which didn't seem to fall at all. In the visual arts, one of the most enduring mysteries was how to represent what we see in front of us in three dimensions on a two-dimensional surface. In both cases, people struggled for centuries to come to an understanding of the phenomena. Even the most baffling mysteries, though, eventually crumble under the force of human intelligence. With sufficient thought, a first-level understanding emerges from the

## Hunches, Heuristics, and Algorithmics: A Quick Note

**by Mihnea Moldoveanu**

Being precise about concepts is important, because they are the critical building blocks of any human enterprise, intellectual and otherwise. One way to analyze concepts is to describe the ways in which they are used in particular situations—that is, to highlight their "use cases."

The route out of a mystery begins with a hunch. Hunches are *prelinguistic intuitions*. You are in a dense fog high up in the Rocky Mountains. Darkness is on its way. You can see no more than five feet ahead. As you worry about your next step—and the rest of the way— your peripheral vision "sees" a slanted spruce at 11:00, and you experience a "sense" that you should turn right. If someone were to ask you at the time, "Why do you want to go right?" you could not, of course, answer the question in a way that would seem objective to that person. "Just a hunch," you might say. "Something beyond words." You turn and you get safely to the lodge. You never become aware of the fact that you have seen this tree before, on the way to the woods. The hunch remains a hunch. It remains beyond words but not, obviously, beyond either reason or sense.

---

question at hand. We develop heuristics—rules of thumb—that guide us toward a solution by way of organized exploration of the possibilities.

Consider the falling objects. After a long period of observation and contemplation, human beings in various cultures more or less simultaneously developed the notion of a universal force that tends to pull physical objects earthward. Understanding advanced

Heuristics are *open-ended prompts* to think or act in a particular way. For instance, "Look in the rearview mirror before passing," "Go with the first instinct when trying to decide if someone is lying to you in a face-to-face interaction" (this is a heuristic that recognizes the value of a hunch), or "Buyer beware!" Heuristics offer no *guarantee* that using them produces a certain result. Rather, they contain the vague promise that, all things being equal, using the heuristic in the context it is meant for *may*, or on average, *will* be better for you than not using it. Heuristics are different from hunches in that they are *explicit*: they bring intuitions to language.

Algorithms are *certified production processes*. They *guarantee* that, in the absence of intervention or complete anomaly, following the sequence of steps they embody will produce a particular result. For instance, an algorithm (PRIME_SEARCH) designed to figure out if a given number is a prime number—by brute force—will systematically try to divide that number by every number smaller than itself and return the answer "PRIME" if no divisor is found and "Divisor = . . ." if a divisor is found. Algorithms differ from heuristics in that they offer a *performance guarantee* that comes along with using them: you cannot use the algorithm PRIME_SEARCH on the number 209870987403987 and *not* get an answer, *except* if some catastrophe intervenes and stops you from executing the steps prescribed by the algorithm.

from a mystery—why do things fall to earth?—to a heuristic or a rule of thumb for explaining why things fall: a force we call gravity causes things to fall to earth.

In art, after literally centuries of questioning and experimentation, the heuristic of perspective emerged as a solution to the mystery of three-dimensional representation. First, in about the fifth century BC, came a tool called *skenographia*, which historians con-jecture was developed by Greek dramatists to make their sets appear to have depth. A heuristic had begun to emerge.

Heuristics represent an incomplete yet distinctly advanced understanding of what was previously a mystery. But that under-standing is unequally distributed. Some people remain stuck in the world of mystery, while others master its heuristics. The beauty of heuristics is that they guide us toward a solution by way of organized exploration of the possibilities. With a heuristic to guide his further thought and consideration, the great scientist Sir Isaac Newton derived precise rules for determining how fast an object will fall under any circumstance. Newton's rule—that an object dropped from any height will accelerate at a constant rate of 32 feet per second squared—advanced the understanding of gravity to the third stage, the algorithm. An algorithm is an explicit, step-by-step procedure for solving a problem. Algo-rithms take the loose, unregimented heuristics—which take considerable thought and nuance to employ—and simplify, struc-turalize, and codify them to the degree that anyone with access to the algorithm can deploy it with more or less equal efficiency.

As with gravity, the algorithm for perspective took centuries to develop. By the eleventh century AD, early physicists had arrived at the understanding that the conical shape of the eye influences how we see three-dimensional objects. A few centuries later, the Florentine painter and architect Filippo Brunelleschi studied the heuristic until he innovated a repeatable method—an algorithm—that allowed him and other artists to reliably create the illusion of three-dimensional space.

As understanding moves from mystery to heuristic to algo-rithm, extraneous information is pared away; the complexities of the world are mastered through simplification. That is why my graphic model of the advance of knowledge is a funnel that tapers as knowledge moves through its stages of refinement. The gain in understanding comes from picking salient features of the environment and out of them constructing a causal explanation of the mystery. From the inchoate phenomenon of falling objects came the concept of a universal force that pulls things earthward, which in turn was painstakingly developed, through trial and error, into a simple formula that described the unchanging properties of this once-mysterious force.

There's significant value to pushing knowledge to the algorithm stage. It is quite handy to have at one's disposal a logical, arithmetic, or computational procedure that, if correctly applied, guarantees success. When Brunelleschi created the precise "vanishing point" algorithm for perspective during the first two decades of the fifteenth century, he provided a significant advantage to the Florentine artistic community until the algorithm became more widely disseminated and understood.

The ultimate destination of algorithms as of the late twentieth century is computer code. Once knowledge has been pushed to a logical, arithmetic, or computational procedure, it can be reduced to software. Armed with the algorithm for gravity, clever engineers at Honeywell were able to create autopilot systems for giant commercial aircraft so that they could be made to fall out of the sky in a passenger-friendly fashion without human intervention. And what about Brunelleschi's algorithm for perspective? Computers now use the three-dimensional data transferred from a camera to spit out a two-dimensional representation of it based on the formulas handed down by Brunelleschi and codified in matrix-multiplication software.

Of course, not every mystery can become an algorithm; not all logic can be pushed through to the end of the funnel. Consider the mystery of the oldest art, music. How can certain arrangements of notes, timbres, and rhythms have such a profound effect on our emotions, and how can we harness that power to soothe or rouse our listeners? Norman Greenbaum stumbled on the answer to that mystery once and once only, coming up with the 1969 smash "Spirit in the Sky." Wildly catchy and instantly recognizable, the song continues to spin off royalties that provide Greenbaum with a comfortable living. But the mystery of the hit song remains just that for Greenbaum. He has never produced a follow-up to the fuzzed-up hippie spirituality of "Spirit in the Sky."

Contrast Greenbaum's career with that of U2, the band that developed a heuristic—a way of understanding the world and conveying that understanding through harmony, melody, and rhythm—that enables it to write songs that resonate with millions of people worldwide, not once but over and over. From the release of the earnest, anthemic album *Boy* in 1980 to the eclectic pleasures of *Achtung Baby* in 1991, U2's mastery of heuristics produced a string of industry awards and top-forty hits. But when the band consciously stepped away from the heuristic that had served it so well—experimenting with techno, dance, and electronica on *Zooropa* and *Pop*—fans promptly voted with their feet. When, in 2000, the band reunited with producers Brian Eno and Daniel Lanois to record *All That You Can't Leave Behind*, it also returned to its pre-*Zooropa* heuristic, leading to Bono's famous remark at that year's Grammy Awards: "The whole year has been quite humbling," he said. "Going back to scratch, reapplying for the job.

What job? The best-band-in-the-world job."[2] The heuristic still worked; *Rolling Stone* called *All That You Can't Leave Behind* U2's third masterpiece (after *The Joshua Tree* and *Achtung Baby*).[3]

Yet even U2's greatest albums contain some forgettable songs; its mastery of the heuristics of the pop song falls short of a sure-fire algorithmic formula. The occasional failures of a serial hit maker like U2 tell us something important about heuristics: they don't guarantee success. Heuristics can do no more than increase the probability of getting to a successful outcome or at least getting there more quickly.

Thus far at least, pop music has proven resistant to advance from heuristic to algorithm. But there have been movements in that direction: in the late 1970s, musical innovators like producer Brian Eno experimented with the sound of the human heart and determined that songs with a synthesized heartbeat as their rhythm track are instinctively enjoyed by listeners, no matter what musical setting sits atop the heartbeat. As a producer, he was able to help bands turn out hits in a variety of genres, from the jittery dance-pop of Talking Heads' "Once in a Lifetime" to the orchestral strings of Coldplay's "Viva la Vida" to those massively successful U2 albums. Other producers in search of a success algorithm created a succession of disposable boy bands, pop princesses, or lip-synching electro-pop acts like Milli Vanilli. And even now we have the mass populism of Simon Fuller's *American Idol*, which has produced bona fide stars in Kelly Clarkson and Carrie Underwood, and a few forgettable flashes in the pan. The algorithm remains elusive. There is still nothing close to a formula for producing consistent success in the music business. Yet.

## Back to McDonald's

Incongruous as it might sound, the McDonald brothers and Ray Kroc followed the same path that Newton and Brunelleschi trod as they built their business from a single drive-in to a global enterprise. Their journey began with the question that so perplexed the McDonald brothers as they watched a new culture grow up around them: what and how did the mobile, leisured, mass middle class of southern California want to eat? That was their mystery.

The brothers devised an answer by focusing on a specific facet of that emerging culture—the consumers' desired out-of-home eating experience. The heuristic they developed—a quick-service restaurant with strictly limited menu options—emerged when they narrowed the field of possibilities to a manageable set of salient features. In doing so, the McDonald brothers discovered a way to create value from their understanding of their world.

Kroc then picked up the baton, driving that understanding—that heuristic—all the way to an algorithm by continuing to cut away vast tracts of possibility. Hamburgers could be charbroiled or pressure-cooked. The menu could be broad or narrow. Restaurants could be smaller or larger. Ultimately, Kroc plucked one answer along innumerable dimensions to construct McDonald's defining algorithm. Once that algorithm was in place, Kroc pushed it as far as it would go, adapting its elements to changing markets and economic conditions, but leaving its essential outlines unchanged.

## The Creation of Value in Business

The McDonald's story illustrates important elements of the dynamics of the march of knowledge from mystery to heuristic to

algorithm: the paring away of information and the simplification of the world's complexities. The gain in understanding comes from picking out salient features of the environment and out of them building a causal understanding of it: "I think that Californians would like a quick-service hamburger joint." The heuristic doesn't attempt an encyclopedic understanding of the new Californian beach culture and how the freeway system brought it into being. It focuses instead on a specific facet of that culture: the consumers' desired out-of-home eating experience.

To create an algorithm from that heuristic requires clear-cutting more vast tracts of possibility. Ultimately, one answer along innumerable dimensions had to be plucked to provide McDonald's' defining algorithm. Judgment was removed, possibilities were removed, and variety was removed.

What is the value to a business of driving through the knowledge funnel from mystery to heuristic to algorithm? The reward is a massive gain in efficiency. By paring away possibilities from the mystery of what and how Californians want to eat to the limited menu, drive-through, quick-service burger joint, the McDonald brothers could focus on a few important things and replicate the model several times over, extending its success.

When Kroc converted the heuristic into a precise algorithm, he was able to scale the chain to a size previously unimaginable. Restaurant site selection followed an efficient algorithm, so sites could be found and developed quickly in each desired locale. Staffing the restaurant was easy, because the procedures for hiring the unskilled labor needed were precisely laid out and the new employees could be readily taught the precise in-restaurant procedures from comprehensive manuals. Supply of food and beverage items to the new restaurant could be easily added to the precisely organized supply chain, making that supply chain even higher scale and more efficient.

By solving the mystery before its competitors, McDonald's created an efficiency advantage. By honing and refining the heuristic, it extended that efficiency advantage. By converting that heuristic to algorithm, new owner Kroc drove the efficiency advantage still further ahead of its competitors, creating an enterprise worth billions of dollars—all from one new-style burger joint.

## A Fine Balance

Matching McDonald's accomplishment—and that of every other organization that creates value across the knowledge funnel—requires two very different activities: *moving across the knowledge stages* of the funnel from mystery to heuristic and heuristic to algorithm and *operating within each knowledge stage* of the funnel by honing and refining an existing heuristic or algorithm. We can map these two different activities onto the theories of the great management theorist James March, who posited that organizations may engage primarily in *exploration*, the search for new knowledge (in our terms, seeking movement across the knowledge stages), or *exploitation*, the maximization of payoff from existing knowledge (refinement within a knowledge stage).[4] Both activities can create enormous value, and both are critical to the success of any business organization. But they are hard to engage in simultaneously; most often, organizations choose to focus on one activity, either exploration or exploitation, to the exclusion of the other and to their own detriment.

An organization exclusively dedicated to exploration will expire in relatively short order. Typically, exploration alone will not generate the returns needed to fund further exploration. Imagine Norman Greenbaum as a corporation. After the one random incident of successful intuitive thinking, of exploration, that created "Spirit in the Sky," Greenbaum Inc. would have gone bust waiting for the next chance event—which never happened. Devotion to exploration is *the invention of business*, a risky proposition and the reason that nine of ten entrepreneurial start-ups expire in less than two years. Exploration alone is unstable business.

On the other hand, many organizations flip quickly from an early exploration phase—the generation of the founding idea behind the business—to the steady exploitation of that idea, never returning to exploration. These organizations, solely dedicated to exploitation, might last somewhat longer than exploration-only businesses, but the business that creates value only through exploitation will exhaust itself in due course. It can't keep exploiting the same piece of knowledge forever. If it tries to do so, the cost to the business can be devastating.

The exploitation of knowledge within a given stage—that is, running an existing heuristic, gently honing and refining it, but not seeking to move knowledge to an algorithm or running an existing algorithm and not seeking to explore the next mystery— is the *administration of business*. A high-end Wall Street law firm runs the legal-services heuristic over and over; McDonald's runs the fast-food algorithm over and over. That is a far different activity from the exploration that drives knowledge from one stage to the next—from mystery to heuristic, from heuristic to algorithm. (See table 1-1.)

**TABLE 1-1**

## Characteristics of exploration and exploitation

|  | Exploration | Exploitation |
|---|---|---|
| Organizational focus | The invention of business | The administration of business |
| Overriding goal | Dynamically moving from the current knowledge stage to the next | Systematically honing and refining within the current knowledge stage |
| Driving forces | Intuition, feeling, hypotheses about the future, originality | Analysis, reasoning, data from the past, mastery |
| Future orientation | Long-term | Short-term |
| Progress | Uneven, scattered, characterized by false starts and significant leaps forward | Accomplished by measured, careful incremental steps |
| Risk and reward | High risk, uncertain but potentially high reward | Minimal risk, predictable but smaller rewards |
| Challenge | Failure to consolidate and exploit returns | Exhaustion and obsolescence |

The vast majority of businesses follow a common path. The company is birthed through a creative act that converts a mystery to a heuristic through intuitive thinking. It then hones and refines that heuristic through increasingly pervasive analytical thinking and enters a long phase in which the administration of business dominates. And in due course, a competitor stares at the mystery that provided the spark for this company, comes up with a more powerful heuristic, and supplants the original business.

A small fraction of those companies generate a second intuitive breakthrough—often, as in the case of McDonald's, from a new owner rather than the original entrepreneur—and drive the heuristic to algorithm. These exceptional companies grow to massive size, thanks to the efficiency advantage gained over competitors left behind in the heuristic stage. But they too can fall prey to a new competitor that returns to the original mystery and generates a new heuristic—one powerful enough to overcome even the enormous efficiency advantages of the algorithm. They too can be supplanted in due course.

## Picking Up the Option

The business that remains at one stage in the knowledge funnel fails to capitalize on the option created when knowledge is advanced quickly through the funnel. It misses the opportunity to delve into the next mystery and push that mystery through the funnel ahead of the competition. To exploit that opportunity, a company can choose to redeploy the personnel who successfully tackled the last mystery and advanced knowledge along the funnel. By putting these resources to work on new mysteries, the company both defends its current position and goes on the offensive by exploring new opportunities.

McDonald's more recent history provides a useful illustration. After its transition from the drive-in heuristic to the quick-service restaurant algorithm, McDonald's grew big and strong exploiting that algorithm with burgers, fries, and shakes. But by the 1990s, it had lost touch with its consumers and what they wanted in the way of fast food; its original solution to that mystery had grown stale with time. The company's management was so busy running its algorithm that it failed to grasp that many consumers wanted the fast turnaround that is McDonald's byword, but with menu offerings that were healthier or more diverse than pressure-cooked beef, deep-fried potatoes, and sugared milk. Many other chains, from Taco Bell to Subway, explored the mystery of what those consumers wanted, and their solutions drove McDonald's into a tailspin.

Playing defense is essential because there are multiple paths out of virtually any mystery. McDonald's chose one route out of the mystery and drove it to an algorithm. But when it settled at that algorithm, it gave its rivals an opening to develop alternative solutions to the mystery. Subway, for example, retained the quick-service component, but replaced burgers and fries with submarine sandwiches and fresh, healthful ingredients.

In doing so, Subway took advantage of the blind spot created on McDonald's path through the knowledge funnel. Remember that as an idea moves through the funnel, information is shaved away. Some of that seemingly extraneous information can in fact prove crucial to the solution of the next mystery. Early on, McDonald's left health issues by the wayside. Subway made healthy eating the centerpiece of its value proposition, touting its fresh ingredients and low-fat specialties in response to consumers' increasing concerns about unhealthy fast food. McDonald's has subsequently made halting progress toward a healthier menu, but its struggles point to the difficulty that companies have in doubling back along the knowledge funnel.

Other companies can spare themselves similar anguish by using the cost savings generated from pushing their current activities through the knowledge funnel to revisit the mystery whose initial solution drove its original business model. By reengaging with the mystery and considering information sliced away during the previous trip through the funnel, a company can avoid being blindsided, as McDonald's was by Subway. Only when McDonald's began to explore new approaches to satisfying the consumers' changing desires did it start to climb out of its trough.

The company that gains efficiencies by pushing current knowledge through the funnel also gains an offensive advantage. It can redeploy the savings and redirect its freed-up personnel toward consideration of entirely new mysteries. Procter & Gamble realized enormous efficiencies by refining its knowledge of household cleaning products. The equity generated by those efficiencies was deployed toward the mystery of baby diapering. The result: Pampers, now one of P&G's biggest businesses. Only fifty years ago it was a complete mystery. In other words, P&G used the equity realized by becoming more efficient to pursue innovation. It exploited the gains of previous advances to fund its exploration of new mysteries.

## Design Thinking and the Design of Business

Very few companies balance exploration and exploitation by continuously looking back up the knowledge funnel to the next salient mystery (or back to the original mystery) and driving across the knowledge funnel, in a steadily cycling process. These few businesses come to be defined by their balanced approach. They become design-thinking businesses.

Why do so many companies fall into the trap of choosing either exploration or exploitation, rather than balancing both? The reason, I believe, is that as companies grow, they become more comfortable with the administration of business. They like and encourage analytical thinking. They embrace a very specific way of arguing and thinking that includes a highly restrictive definition of what constitutes reasonable grounds for moving ahead with a project, a very narrow definition of proof. For analytical thinking, all proof emanates from the past—a general rule handed down from the past, or a set of observations of events or behaviors that have already happened. The average manager has been trained and rewarded to look to the past for proof before making the big decisions.

And to these analytically trained managers, the alternative appears quite frightening: the knowing without the reasoning of intuitive thinking. It is no wonder that organizations slowly but surely shift their structures, processes, and cultures to be friendly to only analytical thinking and, without realizing it, to only exploitation of existing knowledge. Their goal is not to drive out innovation but rather to protect the organization against the randomness of intuitive thinking. They do not realize that they worship at the altar of *reliability*, a concept that I will return to in chapter 2. But drive out innovation they do. It is a trap and a pernicious one.

The answer is not to try to get corporations to embrace the randomness of intuitive thinking and eschew analytical thinking entirely. They just won't do it: it is too scary. What's more, analytical thinking is absolutely essential to the exploitation of existing knowledge. No, we cannot do without analytical thinking or intuitive thinking entirely.

The answer lies in embracing a third form of thinking—design thinking—that helps a company both hone and refine within the existing knowledge stage and generate the leap from stage to stage, continuously, in a process I call *the design of business*. I will explore design thinking at length in chapter 3. For now, let me say that at the heart of design thinking is abductive logic, a concept originated by turn-of-the-twentieth-century philosopher Charles Sanders Peirce. His important insight was that it is not possible to prove any new thought, concept, or idea *in advance*: all new ideas can be validated only through the unfolding of future events. To advance knowledge, we must turn away from our standard definitions of proof—and from the false certainty of the past—and instead stare into a mystery to ask what could be. The answer, Peirce said, would come through making a "logical leap of the mind" or an "inference to the best explanation" to imagine a heuristic for understanding the mystery.

The McDonald brothers didn't know that their Speedee Service System would work. They had imperfect data, but not irrelevant data. They knew that carhop restaurants had the appeal of relatively quick service, but had some drawbacks—loitering toughs and cold food. Their logical leap, their inference, was that patrons liked the basic concept but would like it a lot more if the restaurant were a drive-through with a narrower, more standardized menu.

The brothers had no "proof," but they did not lack logic. At the time a heuristic is first tentatively proposed, no one can prove whether it is useful or valid at all. Proof comes only if the heuristic is tried and found to be helpful in producing the desired, or valid, result. The same holds for turning the heuristic into an algorithm. Neither of these steps into new knowledge can be proved in advance; all are validated—or not—through the passage of time.

As such, abductive logic sits squarely between the past-data-driven world of analytical thinking and the knowing-without-reasoning world of intuitive thinking. Rather than being confined to regressing the past to hone and refine within the current knowledge stage, the design thinker can add abductive logic to the reasoning repertoire to drive the organization through the knowledge funnel. And rather than being confined to the knowing without reasoning of intuitive thinking, the design thinker uses an explicit form of logic and a process that, while less certain and clear than analytical thinking, has promise for producing advances with greater consistency and replicability than pure intuition.

The design thinker therefore enables the organization to balance exploration and exploitation, invention of business and administration of business, and originality and mastery. Design thinking powers the design of business, the directed movement of a business through the knowledge funnel from mystery to heuristic to algorithm and then the utilization of the resulting efficiencies to tackle the next mystery and the next and the next. The velocity of movement through the knowledge funnel, powered by design thinking, is the most powerful formula for competitive advantage in the twenty-first century.

To get there, businesses must acknowledge that they implicitly favor exploitation over exploration, because most businesses, whether they know it or not, favor *reliability* over *validity*. In the next chapter, we will examine those concepts in detail and investigate the forces that converge to reinforce an organizational bias toward reliability. Subsequent chapters will deepen our understanding of the contrasting modes of logic that produce exploration and exploitation, and the implications of both for the way we work. Most firms are dominated by declarative logic, or deductive and inductive reasoning (the logic of what should be or is operative). But new knowledge comes about by way of abductive reasoning, the logic of what might be. I offer a guide to developing the capacity for abductive reasoning—the essential core capacity for design thinkers—in the individual and the organization.

## A Different Kind of Organization

A different kind of thinking demands a different way of organizing work. Reliability-oriented firms view applying a heuristic or running an algorithm on a continuous basis as their overarching task. So they build up permanent departments staffed by fungible people in permanent slots. They devote the bulk of their energies and resources to rigorous planning and strict budgets. Those processes, which are applications of inductive and deductive logic, drive out initiatives that can't produce near-certain future outcomes.

To balance administration and invention, a business needs to shift the weighting of its structure, processes, and culture. While some aspects of the organization can and should continue to be structured as permanent jobs or tasks, significant parts of the organization should be structured as projects—that is, with teams and processes designed to move knowledge forward a stage—with a definite end point. While planning and budget management can't be thrown out the window, they have to be loosened to incorporate initiatives and investments whose outcomes can't be predicted in advance. And culturally, it's imperative that people know it is safe and rewarding to bring forward an abductive argument.

## A Different Kind of Leader

Without committed leadership, no business can realize the structural, process, and cultural adjustments needed to become a design-thinking organization. Given the enticing short-term financial rewards of reliability, most organizations will pursue reliability out of simple self-interest. But given those same rewards, validity has a good chance of being squeezed out if someone at the very top of the organization does not champion its value. CEOs must learn to think of themselves as the organization's balancing force—the promoter of both exploitation and exploration, of both administration and invention.

The CEO can perform that function in a number of different but successful ways. Some CEOs, such as Guy Laliberté, founder of Cirque du Soleil, and Mike Lazaridis, founder of Research In Motion, the company that gave the world the BlackBerry, take it on themselves to lead the search for innovation. Laliberté spearheads the design of circuses the likes of which the world has never seen before. Lazaridis keeps creating new devices that define the future of mobile communications. Both drive their organizations forward by taking the lead in moving knowledge forward.

At the other end of the spectrum, we find CEOs who build design-friendly organizations. Procter & Gamble's A. G. Lafley is the poster boy for transforming a large, reliability-biased enterprise into a design-friendly organization that maintains a balance between analytical thinking and abductive reasoning. James Hackett of Steelcase acquired the design firm IDEO to infuse design thinking across the entire Steelcase organization.[5]

Between the extremes represented by Laliberté and Lazaridis at one end and Hackett and Lafley at the other, there are numerous intermediate alternatives. Steve Jobs, for instance, cofounder and returned CEO of Apple Inc., is probably the CEO most widely viewed as a design thinker, thanks to elegant, customer-pleasing products like the Macintosh, iMac, iPod, and iPhone, among many others. But he is not the solitary design genius of popular imagination. It was Apple's designers, led by Jonathan Ive, who realized those innovative products. Jobs played a different, equally crucial role: he created an organization that placed "insanely great" design at the top of its hierarchy of values, and he gave the green light to spend the resources necessary to make lasting successes of his designers' innovations.

## A Different You

But what if you are not a CEO? Worse, what if the CEO you work for doesn't have the first clue about the importance of design thinking and the need to encourage it? Are you then powerless to improve your circumstances and your organization's prospects?

Definitely not. You are far from powerless, and you are anything but alone. The business world is dominated by reliability. But that need not impede your efforts to sharpen your own design-thinking capability. While you may have to fight your organization's baked-in biases against design thinking, the effort will help you sharpen your innovation skills and prepare you to be your company's champion of design.

To become a design thinker, you must develop the *stance, tools,* and *experiences* that facilitate design thinking. Stance is your view of the world and your role in it. Tools are the models that you use to understand your world and organize your thinking. Experiences are what build and develop your skills and sensitivities over time.

Rather than being cowed by a reliability-oriented world and becoming a prisoner of it, the design thinker develops a stance that puts a priority on seeking validity and making advances in knowledge, even if that stance places the thinker at odds with the organization's culture. In addition to mastering tools for analyzing the past and using that analysis to predict the future, the design thinker develops the capacity for observation, for seeing features that others may miss. The design thinker, in the words of novelist Saul Bellow, is "a first-class noticer."[6]

Along with developing tools for honing and refining the status quo, design thinkers develop tools for moving knowledge forward. They build their capacity for the unique configuration of designs that transform their insights into viable business offerings. And design thinkers use their experiences to deepen their mastery of the current knowledge domain and exercise originality in moving knowledge forward to the next stage. In combination, this approach to your stance, tools, and experiences will create a virtuous cycle, reinforcing your design-thinking approach over time.

Toward the end of the book, I will return to advice for the individual design thinker. First, though, let us turn our attention to the organization and to the powerful currents that the design thinker must swim against to transform it. We need to understand how reliability, which first appears to ensure success for any business that cultivates it to its highest point, turns out to be the chief limiter of success. And how validity, which at first seems to be the enemy of reliability, is the force that, when paired with reliability, creates a winning advantage.

CHAPTER 2

# The Reliability Bias

*Why Advancing Knowledge Is So Hard*

IN THE SPRING of 2008, I met an enthusiastic and gregarious geneticist named Stephen Scherer, from Toronto's world-renowned Hospital for Sick Children. Dr. Scherer, it turns out, is one of world's leading researchers into autism, or to be more precise, into autism spectrum disorder (ASD). The study of autism is a relatively young field, with a body of research going back only seventy years or so. The somewhat scattered nature of the research is representative of the challenges faced by the investigators of any mystery. With a mystery, it is difficult to know where to start. What is this condition? Where does it originate? How does it operate? What makes children with ASD behave as they do? Is it the result of a virus? Is it the way their parents treat them? Is it a response to environmental conditions, diet, or even the vaccinations administered to them in infancy? Is it genetic? How can a researcher even begin to think about understanding and treating this mysterious disorder?

With so much unknown, investigators have to consider every possible contributor to the condition, because they do not yet know what to leave out. Anything omitted might turn out to be a key to unlocking the mystery. With little to go on, investigators typically seek a pattern in the chaos and look deeply into that pattern for answers. Based on our brief conversation, I began to suspect that Scherer approached his mystery—and the search for patterns within it—a little differently and perhaps more successfully than most of us do. What sets Scherer apart, I thought, is that he looks for patterns in the data that other researchers discard as extraneous.

Scherer's unconventional approach has met with unconventional success. He was just forty-four years old when I sat with him at an awards dinner, where he was to receive the evening's capstone award. Yet he already had more than 240 peer-reviewed journal articles on his résumé, cited by other scholars more than fifteen thousand times. His list of awards is too long to recite.[1] I was so intrigued by Scherer's work and methods that I arranged to meet him again at his laboratory. I wanted to learn how he thinks about turning medical mysteries into heuristics and algorithms.

We started the meeting in his office, where I learned more about what the self-deprecating Scherer calls his "garbage can approach." Scherer credits his breakthroughs in understanding ASD to his focus on data that others tend to toss into the trash. He believes that the answers to mysteries can often be found in the "outlier" data that does not seem to fit comfortably within one of the categories he or others have constructed. To illustrate his point, he drew a simple scatter plot diagram and then drew large circles around the dots that seemed to fit together. Finally, he pointed to a few dots farthest removed from the clusters of data. "These are the really interesting things," he said. "These are the guys that we study."[2]

To help me understand more concretely what he was saying, we walked from his office to his laboratory. And what a lab it was. The second we passed through the security door, we stepped out of what felt like a normal office building into the future. There were complex machines stacked high on racking systems as far as I could see. Modern medical research is a capital-intensive game. Scherer showed me a gene microchip high-definition imaging device that he uses to compare DNA sequences from individuals with ASD against control samples from people without the condition. He showed me slides of the results, pointing out the large peaks that indicated missing DNA on the chromosomes of a patient with ASD—deletions that have been studied intensively by scientists around the world. His focus, however, is on the data that other researchers set aside as random, statistically insignificant, or simply not germane.

"Look at this," he said, leaning over a slide of a genetic sequence. "What else do you see besides the peaks? You see all of these other little things. In every experiment, you see these little spurious things come up. Everybody else throws them away." His experience as a geneticist tells him that the discarded data may contain clues to the genetic anomaly underlying ASD. "In genetics," he explained, "nature often protects things through redundancy, complexity, and variability, all of which cloud our resolution for interpretation. So those individual, hard-to-reproduce variations are like a signpost: this is what you should be looking at."

After twenty years of research, Scherer has started to see a pattern emerge from those little differences. With a "logical leap of the mind," he has formulated a heuristic, which is that the key to the mystery is to be found in deletions and duplications in certain genes ("copy number variations," as geneticists call them) found in children with ASD. Those genetic anomalies, he infers, predispose autistic children to have developmental imbalances leading to unique behavioral tendencies including repetitive overanalysis of aspects of their world, such as numerical patterns or arrangements of objects. Rather than process information and move on, as most of us do, these individuals settle on a feature of their mental or physical environment and dig in, obsessively analyzing and reanalyzing the information to the exclusion of the rest of the world. The medical term for this obsessive, repetitive focus is perseveration.

Scherer's heuristic is typical in that it makes no attempt to encompass the width and breadth of the problem at hand. He has left out large tracts of investigative territory, such as possible environmental causes and sections of missing DNA. To wrestle the mystery down to manageable size, he focused on understanding *what* autistic children do. His answer: they overanalyze or perseverate. From there, he examined *why* they do so, and from his discovery of a pattern in seemingly unrelated bits of nonconforming genetic data, he has concluded that the answer is to be found in the copy number variations of people with ASD. By limiting his focus, he has advanced to a working heuristic, while many of his colleagues worldwide are still probing the mystery and cycling through numerous potential angles of attack.

Scherer moved from mystery to heuristic by focusing not on what was common from experiment to experiment—the replicable peaks in the genetic sequence—but by focusing on what was different—the oddball findings that stood out from the others as unexplained and unexpected. As he says, "evolution doesn't tolerate junk for too long, so all data, even the outliers, need to be considered." Ultimately, he was interested not in producing a reliable outcome but a valid one. He wanted to generate a theory on the origins of ASD that would move knowledge forward.

This distinction, between reliability and validity, is at the heart of the innovation dilemma, for medical researchers and businesspeople alike. The challenge is how to balance the irresolvable tension between operating within the current knowledge stage and moving through the knowledge funnel. The tension can't be fully resolved but only balanced and managed, because reliability and validity are inherently incompatible.

The goal of *reliability* is to produce consistent, predictable outcomes. A perfectly reliable blood-testing procedure would produce *the same test results* each of a hundred times, if a blood sample were divided into a hundred portions and tested successively using the procedure. A perfectly reliable political poll would produce the same result from five different random samples of voters. Reliability, in this context, is achieved by narrowing the scope of the test to what can be measured in a replicable, quantitative way and by eliminating as much subjectivity, judgment, and bias as possible.

The goal of *validity,* on the other hand, is to produce outcomes that meet a desired objective. A perfectly valid system produces a result that is shown, through the passage of time, to be *correct*. A valid blood test is one that assesses whether that the subject actually *has* hepatitis B or not. A perfectly valid political poll would predict in advance the winner of the election and the winning percentage. Validity is difficult to achieve with only quantitative measures, because those measures strip away nuance and context. Typically, to achieve a valid outcome, one must incorporate some aspects of the subjectivity and judgment that are eschewed in the quest for a reliable outcome.

To illustrate the distinction between reliability and validity a little more clearly, let's return to medical research, Scherer's field. Scherer was interested in validity, even at the expense of greater reliability. He looked at small differences, rather than big similarities across test results. This emphasis on getting to a valid answer enabled him to move from one stage of the knowledge funnel (mystery) to the next (heuristic). But consider the kind of large-scale, groundbreaking work that requires hundreds of participants around the world to work together, refining knowledge within one stage. Here, reliability would be paramount, as it was in the execution of the Human Genome Project.

The Human Genome Project, the great global medical project of the past decade, was a publicly funded endeavor (alongside a parallel, privately funded effort headed by Dr. J. Craig Venter, a pioneer in gene-sequencing technology) that used donor DNA from more than seven hundred anonymous individuals to create a single mosaic sequence representative of universal human DNA.[3] The model constructed from that massive data set smoothed out individual differences to assemble a merged sequence meant to reflect the genetic information we all have in common. Note that by creating a seven-hundred-person composite, the effort wiped out every piece of "garbage can" data that Scherer would have used to establish his findings. That is a key price of reliability: the simplification or conformity that enables consistent replicability also leaves out knowledge that is necessary for greater validity.

Unlike Scherer's work, which to date has progressed along the knowledge funnel only from mystery to heuristic, the Human Genome Project represented the careful application and refinement of an algorithm. That is in fact what made the project possible. The Human Genome Project scientists reduced the task of gene sequencing to a specific algorithm, which enabled them to assign research teams worldwide the task of applying that sequencing algorithm to a particular piece of the overall genome. This would not have been possible if the sequencing technique had remained a heuristic; in that case, the teams would have utilized many different approaches based on their expert judgment in applying the heuristic. Operating the relatively efficient and clear algorithm, on the other hand, required little application of judgment.

While it was an epic and mammoth project, there was little doubt that the researchers would eventually succeed in assembling the human genetic model because their method was reliable. The real question was how soon they would complete the sequence. Thanks in part to competitive pressure from Venter's parallel project, the Human Genome Project finished ahead of schedule. In scientific research as in business, pushing knowledge from heuristic to algorithm generates impressive efficiencies.

The Human Genome Project has its parallels in the business world, where large groups of highly trained people employ algorithms in pursuit of reliable results. Case in point: today's complex, elaborate, firmwide software. Enterprise resource planning (ERP) systems keep track of all corporate data in a single database and spit out comprehensive reports on everything from inventory levels to sales by product to cost absorption by area. Customer relationship management (CRM) systems purport to ensure that a company knows exactly who its customers are, what each is buying, and what more it could sell to them. Six Sigma programs and total quality management (TQM) systems knock the waste out of an organization's systems, and knowledge management (KM) systems (attempt to) organize all the knowledge in a corporation. Those and other tools enable the modern corporation to crunch data objectively and extrapolate from the past to make "scientific" predictions about the future, all part of the quest for reliability.

Commercial enterprises seek validity too, of course, usually classifying the activity as research and development. Pharmaceutical companies spend billions of dollars each year staring into the mysteries of diseases. Consumer packaged-goods companies like Unilever and Colgate spend billions each year to explore the mysteries of consumer desires and the products that might satisfy them. Similar efforts are under way at information technology companies, medical device companies, and other companies in research-intensive sectors. In each case, their inquiries are considered high-risk activity, because they lack a formal production process. The corporation cannot define the resources or time frame required to solve the mystery, which means that debt financing cannot be used as a source of funding for the exploration. Debt must to be paid back on a predetermined schedule, and thus exploration, which has no schedule, requires equity financing, which has no fixed schedule for paying equity providers or even any assurance that the equity providers will ever be repaid. Given this dynamic, it's no wonder that the business world chooses reliability over validity.

## Why Reliability Rules

In 2007, I attended a dinner at which Martin Baily, former chairman of President Bill Clinton's Council of Economic Advisors, presented McKinsey & Company's "Ten Trends to Watch" for the next decade. Baily was speaking in his capacity as senior adviser to the McKinsey Global Institute (MGI), its associated think tank. He rattled his way through the list, highlighting shifts in centers of economic activity, consumer trends, and corporate oversight. It was the ninth item on the list that really captured my attention. At that point, Baily eloquently and enthusiastically described how scientific management would triumph over gut instinct and intuition.

Interest piqued, I visited the McKinsey Web site the next morning to learn more. Posted there was an article by Ian Davis (then McKinsey's worldwide managing director) and his colleague Elizabeth Stephenson entitled, "Ten Trends to Watch in 2006." "Management," the authors wrote, "will go from art to science. Bigger, more complex companies demand new tools to run and manage them. Indeed, improved technology and statistical-control tools have given rise to new management approaches that make even mega-institutions viable. Long gone is the day of the 'gut instinct' management style," they continued. "Today's business leaders are adopting algorithmic decision-making techniques and using highly sophisticated software to run their organizations. Scientific management is moving from a skill that creates competitive advantage to an ante that gives companies the right to play the game."[4]

The smart and capable McKinsey folks are far from the only ones casting intuition into the dustbin of history. Many businesses increasingly rely on algorithm-based decision-making and decision-support software. They become highly skilled at using algorithms to produce outcomes that are *reliable,* that is, consistent and predictable. But I am troubled by this tendency and by the confidence of thinkers like Baily and Davis that the cultivation of reliability represents the one true course to business success. Companies that devote all their resources to reliability lack the tools to pursue outcomes that are *valid,* that is, that produce a desired result. Indeed, many organizations see no value at all in valid outcomes. Little wonder, then, that those same organizations don't know how to manage validity-seeking activities to generate lasting business value.

Reliability-oriented management systems are, as the McKinsey article rightly observed, vital to the operation of any large organization. But they are no panacea. An ERP system can provide useful real-time data to track whether resources are being used efficiently, but it cannot generate a robust strategy. CRM systems put a wealth of data at the fingertips of customer-service reps, but data is no substitute for intimacy, as corporations discover when customers complain that the systems make them feel as if they are buying from Big Brother. Six Sigma and TQM systems drive out waste from the business as currently configured, but they will not generate innovative new business designs. KM systems will (sort of) organize all the knowledge in a corporation, but they cannot produce imaginative breakthroughs. Advances in knowledge emerge from the pursuit of valid results. That pursuit calls for a different set of tools and processes and, indeed, a different sort of organization.

To acknowledge that algorithms have their limitation is not to disparage their very real business value. When a business has sufficiently honed its heuristic knowledge and moved it along the knowledge funnel to an algorithm, costs fall and efficiency increases, to the benefit of the organization and its stakeholders. But an organization that defines itself as being primarily or exclusively in the business of running algorithms is taking a high risk, even though highly reliable processes are supposed to eliminate uncertainty. What organizations dedicated to running reliable algorithms often fail to realize is that while they reduce the risk of small variations in their businesses, they increase the risk of cataclysmic events that occur when the future no longer resembles the past and the algorithm is no longer relevant or useful.

A business that is overweighted toward reliability will erect organizational structures, processes, and norms that drive out the pursuit of valid answers to new questions. It fails to balance its pursuit of reliability with the equally important pursuit of validity, leaving it ill-positioned to solve mysteries and move knowledge along the funnel. Such organizations inevitably come to see maintenance of the status quo as an end in itself, short-circuiting their ability to design and redesign themselves continuously. This wouldn't be such a big problem if the world never changed; in those circumstances, continuing to replicate the success model would make lots of sense. However, as we all know, the world is continuously changing, and with every change, crucial new mysteries spring up that reliable systems simply won't address or even acknowledge. By implicitly or explicitly focusing on reliability only, organizations deny themselves the immense value that can be unleashed by balancing reliability and validity in a design-thinking organization and expose themselves to the risk of being outflanked by a new entrant. The business that fails to balance reliability and validity will find itself flat-footed when rivals advance knowledge through the funnel.

But why do so many businesses have such a pronounced tilt toward reliability if that tilt does not serve their long-term interest? The short answer is that the modes of reasoning that produce reliable outcomes are familiar to businesspeople from long exposure and experience. The mode of reasoning that produces valid outcomes is sufficiently unfamiliar that it is often seen as no reasoning at all. Given those baseline attitudes, it is no surprise that most firms put reliability at the center of the business universe and drive validity to the margins.

In most large business organizations, three forces converge to enshrine reliability and marginalize validity: the demand that an idea be proved before it is implemented, an aversion to bias, and the constraints of time.

### The Persistence of the Past

The demand for proof might be the most powerful of those forces, dominating as it does senior management's deliberations about allocating capital. Embedded in the verb *prove* are meanings that implicitly privilege reliability over validity. In corporations, to prove something means to look at the past and apply one of two forms of logic—inductive or deductive—to produce a declaration that something is or is not true.

If, in 2007, General Motors marketing executives wanted to prove that the corporation should focus on producing and marketing full-size pickup trucks and SUVs, they could cite sales, margin, and cost and profit data from the previous ten years to inductively prove their case. Indeed, those vehicles had generated the company's highest returns in the past. Alternatively, if executives at PepsiCo wanted to gain approval of a marketing plan, they would invoke a principle established by more than a century of continuous operation: increase market share and profits will follow as night follows day. That is deductive logic—application of a general rule derived from past experience—and Pepsi executives invoke it to prove that if their plan produces market-share growth, it will of necessity increase profits.

Both these forms of analytical logic draw on past experience to predict the future. It is no accident that the future predicted through analytical methods closely resembles the past, differing in degree but not in kind. If a system has produced a consistent result over time—either over such a long period and so universally that it becomes a deductive rule, or over enough repetitions to support a statistically significant induction—it is by definition reliable, and past data can be adduced to prove its reliability.

In an environment that relies primarily on analytical reasoning as a guide to action, past experience carries great argumentative weight. It nearly always prevails against proposals that can only be proven by future events. Because it is so well suited to satisfying the organizational demand for proof, reliability almost always trumps validity. But it is all too often a hollow victory. When the future takes a different course than the path the data predicted for it, all the proofs in the world are unavailing. Just ask the GM executives who invoked data from the recent past to make pickups and SUVs their production and marketing priority in 2008.

## The Attempt to Eliminate Bias

Data, though imperfect as a predictor of the future, prevailed in part because it satisfied another demand of business: that decisions be free of the taint of bias. By eliminating bias and subjective judgment from common business decisions, corporations can achieve massive scale and efficiency honing their decision-making apparatus to an algorithm, indeed, to the ultimate algorithm, computer code. Remember, computers don't exercise judgment. They are fast because they don't think. At any point in time as they process the source code that dictates their operation, they ask only one question: am I looking at a one or a zero? Such algorithms have given the world credit-scoring systems, insurance pricing systems, and targeted marketing systems such as Amazon's product recommendations, all of which process masses of bias-free empirical data to allocate credit, set premium prices, or place product offerings in front of individual consumers.

But the market's response suggests that such reliability-based approaches are less than fully satisfactory. No one can argue that credit-scoring systems and the like show bias or lack objectivity. But that does not make them popular. People who have been subjected to any of these systems feel the depersonalizing, dehumanizing effect of seeing their character and experience reduced to a numerical score. They object to the notion that something as personal as one's tastes in books or music can be reduced to a formula. It is little consolation that the formula is bias-free.

## *The Pressures of Time*

The third reason that reliability tends to trump validity in business settings is, quite simply, time. A reliable system can generate tremendous time savings; once designed, it eliminates the need for subjective and thoughtful analysis by an expensive and time-pressed manager or professional. Hence the appeal of automated asset-allocation systems at investment advisory firms: before new clients even meet an adviser, the clients complete a questionnaire designed to reliably assess their investment horizons, risk tolerance, and investment goals. The data feeds into a program that impersonally graphs the recommended mix of stocks, bonds, and other investments. It takes the massively complex job of understanding individual investment needs out of the hands of the adviser. Where there was once an adviser consulting with clients at length and depth, and then tailoring a portfolio by applying a heuristic and subjective judgment, there is now an algorithm that quickly produces reliable answers.

Of course, the demand for proof, the absence of bias, and the pressures of time affect a good deal more than the forms customers have to fill out. They strongly influence the very shape of the corporation itself, and the structures, processes, and norms that guide its daily activities. If the goal of the reliability-oriented business is to ensure that tomorrow consistently and predictably replicates yesterday, then it follows that the business will be organized as a permanent structure with long-term ongoing job assignments. Daily work will consist of a series of permanent, continuous tasks: make stuff, sell it, ship it, follow up with customers, and service the installed base. There are few if any limited-term projects on

the organizational chart, and for good reason. In most corporations, "special projects" is a euphemism for the purgatory reserved
for terminated executives hunting for a new job.

In such an environment, the organizational goal evolves toward
managing permanent, continuous tasks to the highest possible
level of reliability. Think of General Electric during the Jack
Welch era, when the company's flagship product was not an
industrial turbine or a refrigerator or a medical imaging device
but a quarterly earnings number that reliably met or ever so
slightly exceeded earnings guidance. Because of the environment's demands for reliability, work is only secondarily the business of making stuff and selling it. It is primarily a matter of
ensuring that the existing heuristic or algorithm produces a consistent result time and time again. (See "Counterproductive Pressure from the Public Capital Markets.")

The reliability bias is deeply embedded in organizational
processes related to planning and budgeting, executive skill development, and the use of analytical technology. In all those processes,
conventional wisdom says that reliability equals success. In most
corporations, for example, the first measure of an operation's success is whether it reliably meets a predetermined quantitative
goal: the budget. Anything new and different that threatens the
overriding goal of making budget is rejected out of hand. Constraints such as rising materials costs are equally threatening, as
they add complexity, undermining the algorithm that produces
the desired consistent result.

The managerial skills that are built and rewarded are those of
running heuristics or algorithms to produce reliable outcomes.
Consider the cottage industry that has grown up around Six

Sigma. Six Sigma relentlessly simplifies algorithms to the bare minimum, taking reliability to its logical extreme. Its statistical measures plane away from the algorithm any nuance that would sacrifice consistency of result. Many organizations—most famously, General Electric—promote Six Sigma techniques and reward managers who become Six Sigma "Black Belts." These Black Belts are reliability masters.

In even wider use than Six Sigma is a tool that was virtually unknown to corporate boardrooms just a generation ago: linear regression, a tool that is used for "proving" statistically the relationship between one factor (e.g., store hours) and another (e.g., sales per square foot). Managers prove the value of their ideas by invoking the size of their regression's $R^2$. Proficiency in regression analysis, as well as large-scale analytical systems such as ERP and CRM, are prerequisites for senior executives in corporations. When you consider the amount of resources that individuals and businesses invest to develop those analytical skills, compared to the relatively paltry resources invested in the intuitive skills that produce valid answers, it is easy to see why most corporations tilt so strongly in favor of reliability.

Reinforcing that tilt are organizational norms that govern status and the style of reasoning that the organization considers acceptable. Rewards and high status flow to those managers who analyze past performance to refine heuristics and algorithms, and the highest status and biggest rewards accrue to the executive who reliably runs the most important heuristic or algorithm, importance being measured by revenue and profit. Think of Goldman Sachs's sales and trading heuristic or McDonald's U.S. business algorithm. Managers do their best to dodge tricky smaller

## Counterproductive Pressure from the Public Capital Markets

All too often, companies mismanage the resources freed up by movement along the knowledge funnel. Tragically, the public capital markets encourage this inefficiency, which can be fatal. The public capital markets are reliability-oriented and encourage excessive exploitation, though not necessarily by intention.

The capital markets reward certainty. Nothing is surer to win analysts' favor than a record of delivering predictable revenue and earnings, and nothing is surer to arouse their ire than a failure to meet earnings forecasts. Even a penny's shortfall in quarterly earnings per share can trigger negative analyst reports, downgrades, and sell-offs. For example, on September 25, 2008, Research In Motion announced that its second-quarter profit had risen to 86 cents per share from 50 cents per share the previous year. Profits were $496 million for the quarter; revenue was $2.6 billion. The earnings-per-share results were just one cent below the consensus analyst estimate. How did the market respond? The stock dropped by almost 30 percent, destroying some $16.1 billion in value in a single day.[5]

Analysts don't see the consequences of elevating precision and certainty as the be-all and end-all of business. They fail to recognize their own demand that businesses cease investing in innovative, validity-oriented activities. Remember that mysteries have no production process. Not even the most plugged-in analyst can predict with any certainty when a mystery will yield to a heuristic, or a heuristic to an algorithm. Validity can be demonstrated only by the passage of time. It doesn't happen on strict quarterly schedules, unlike investments in exploiting the current heuristic or algorithm.

The longer-term effect of the capital markets' preference for remaining at the same knowledge stage is stagnation. At some point, exploitation activities will run out of steam, and the company will be outflanked by competitors taking more exploratory approaches. Earnings will stop growing or even decline, and the analysts will savage the company for its lack of innovation. As James March points out, "An organization that engages exclusively in exploitation will ordinarily suffer from obsolescence."[6]

Publicly traded companies have great difficulty resisting the capital markets' pressure to hone and refine within a single knowledge stage. Companies that balance exploitation with exploration, reliability with validity, and refinement with innovation will find themselves targets of heavy criticism from analysts. These analysts think they are being constructive. They're not. They're discouraging the very activity—moving knowledge through the funnel faster than competitors, driving down costs of current activities, and freeing up time and capital to engage in new activities—that creates enduring competitive advantage.

The public capital markets also discourage innovation by demanding that companies divert the savings generated by advancing across the funnel to shareholders. Of course, shareholders have legitimate claim on corporate cash, whether it takes the form of dividends or stock buybacks. But by demanding that they be served first, they work against their own long-term interests. Like the analysts, they prevent the company from achieving the competitive advantage gained from advancing knowledge faster than the competition.

The private capital markets have the opposite effect on companies. The private capital markets like nothing better than a company that relentlessly advances knowledge from one stage to the next, as long as the advance creates value that is captured at the end point of private capital investment, the highly coveted "liquidity event." Yes, private capital seldom avoids failures and write-offs. But there's a reason that the private capital markets are growing much more quickly than the public capital markets. Private capital embraces knowledge advance, while public capital—knowingly or unknowingly—discourages it.

businesses that face complicated mysteries, which are seen as detours to advancement, if not career dead ends.

In such an organization, personal success is achieved by running existing heuristics and algorithms. Self-interest dictates that managers refrain from cycling back to the first stage of the knowledge funnel. The organization's own reward systems and processes practically dictate that it exploit knowledge at its current stage in the funnel, particularly, perhaps, if it is at the heuristic stage.

In corporate settings, high-level heuristics are generally in the hands of highly paid executives or specialists. Out of sheer self-interest, they are reluctant to relinquish their enigmatic and valuable capability. Whether they are brand managers, investment bankers, acquisitions editors, CFOs, research scientists, or star salespeople, they are in a constant tug-of-war with the owners of their company over the spoils of their work. They have the skill—the heuristic inside their heads—and the company has the capital. The company would like maximum compensation for providing the capital. The talent would like maximum compensation for running the heuristic. As long as the talent keeps its heuristic shrouded in priestly secrecy, it can bargain successfully for a bigger share of the value it creates. If the talent were to advance the heuristic to the algorithm stage, the company could hand the specialist's job to a much less expensive person.

In many organizations, including professional service organizations such as law firms, consulting firms, investment firms, and most entertainment and media firms, talent is winning this battle. And the price of maintaining an ongoing monopoly on important heuristics is high. These heuristic-running high priests create a big bottleneck in the middle of the knowledge funnel, blocking the movement forward to algorithm. Their desire to collect monopoly rents sharply limits the speed at which the organization can advance knowledge.

No organization sets out to limit its ability to innovate and create additional value. No board would vote to drive out movement along the knowledge funnel. But to paraphrase Winston Churchill, first we shape our tools and then our tools shape us.[7] The structures, processes, and norms of the contemporary business organization all but condemn it to remain within a single knowledge stage. When a validity-oriented advance comes to an important organizational decision gate, someone in authority inevitably asks reliability-oriented questions: "But can we prove this will work?" or, "How can we be sure of the outcome?" Typically the answers are no, it cannot be proven, and we cannot be sure. So design thinking is suppressed without explicit intent, a victim of organizational bias toward reliability.

## Making Room for Validity

Both reliability and validity are important for an organization. Without validity, an organization has little chance of moving knowledge across the funnel. Without reliability, an organization will struggle to exploit the rewards of its advances. As with exploration and exploitation, the optimal approach to validity and reliability is not to choose but to seek a balance of both. (See figure 2-1.)

The precise method for balancing validity and reliability will vary from situation to situation and from organization to organization. It may be that some areas of an organization (accounting, for example) will emphasize reliable measures, while others (R&D) will embrace valid ones. Still other departments, marketing for instance, may seek to design new measures that in themselves strike a balance,

**FIGURE 2-1**

## The predilection gap

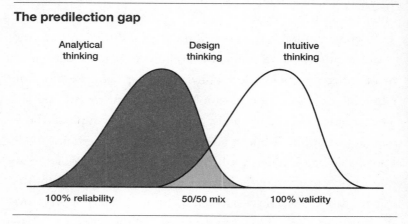

| Analytical thinking | Design thinking | Intuitive thinking |
|---|---|---|

| 100% reliability | 50/50 mix | 100% validity |

incorporating reliable structures around qualitative research methods, for example. But, given that companies have very real and powerful reasons to favor reliability over validity, and that this preference for reliability is often enshrined in the organization's structures, processes, and norms, the challenge will typically be to incorporate a validity orientation into a reliability culture. To do so, the organization must open up new definitions of proof, embrace some degree of subjectivity as not just inevitable but valuable, and acknowledge that getting the right answer is worth taking a little more time. It must open itself up to a new way of thinking. (See "Reliability Versus Validity: A Note on Prediction.") The next chapter will introduce the often-overlooked reasoning skill that is crucial to redressing the imbalance toward reliability and to achieving a productive balance of exploration and exploitation. That skill is abductive reasoning, which drives the intuitive spark that leaps across the gap separating the world as it is from the world as it might be.

# Reliability Versus Validity: A Note on Prediction

### by Mihnea Moldoveanu

Let us start with examining a *reliable* prediction. What could this mean? Well, a reliable prediction, which we'll denote by a sentence, S, about some future event, is one that is produced by a reliable process. A reliable process, in turn, is one that has turned up a reliable prediction N times in the past, where N is a very large number. A reliable prediction of the effects of mortgage rates on housing prices is that they vary in inverse proportion. It is reliable because the process that generated it has *worked* in the past.

Now, what is a *valid* prediction? It is a prediction that turns out to be true. A prediction is always about *the future,* and, as such, it cannot be judged to be valid before the future about which it is predicated actually happens.

The "inductive fallacy" is that of inferring validity from reliability. In its strong (and most pernicious) form, the inductive fallacy states that the reliability of a prediction logically *entails* its validity. So, pre-1999, a reliable prediction would be that high-tech start-up valuations should increase as a large multiple of hits on the fledgling company's Web site and the number of engineers employed by the company. Using this reliable method for predicting firm valuation post September 2000 would, however, have led to an *invalid* prediction and plenty of invalid investments, as it turned out.

The weak form of the inductive fallacy is that the probability of a prediction being valid, given that it is reliable, is greater than the probability of its being invalid, given that it is reliable. Bertrand Russell put this to rest with the simple fable of a chicken who expects (correctly) to be fed every time the farmer appears in the morning, and who predicts (reliably, but not validly) that it will also be fed on (what turns out to be) its last day on Earth, when the farmer comes to chop off its head.

The problem of going from reliability to validity is, of course, the "all things being equal" condition that appears in most experimental reports and empirical study results, which states that the supposed cause-effect relationship supported by the data will be operational in other contexts, "all things being equal." But that is precisely the point of living in an open, uncontrolled system, also known as the world: all things are *not* equal from one experimental run to another. The step that safeguards the transition from reliability to validity is not a simple inferential step but, rather, a far more complex, abductive step. The validity seeker, unlike the reliability seeker, treats past predictive successes as *hypotheses* to be carefully tested before using them to generate predictions that are expected to be valid. Hence, the *real* empiricist is "a first-rate noticer" of precisely the anomalies that would cause him or her to throw out the "all things are equal" assumption.

## CHAPTER 3

# Design Thinking

*How Thinking Like a Designer Can Create*
*Sustainable Advantage*

THE FIRST TIME I VISITED the Research In Motion (RIM) headquarters several years ago, I couldn't find the right building. I'd driven about ninety minutes from Toronto to the twin cities of Kitchener and Waterloo. The landscape was as flat as Kansas, with farms flanking either side of the expansive superhighway. This area of southwestern Ontario strikes a unique balance. Just outside town and off the highway, the buggies and carriages of Old Order Mennonites are still a common sight. They mark a stark contrast to Waterloo itself, a city of about a hundred thousand people. Waterloo, traditionally a sleepy university town, has become a high-tech hub, as scores of technology companies have sprouted up, building on the strength of the renowned engineering program at the University of Waterloo. RIM is one of them.

As I wound my way through the streets of Waterloo, I felt I could have been in Anywhere, North America—a shopping mall here, a power center there, a Chinese restaurant, a section of single-family houses, several Starbucks. Eventually I found 176 Columbia Street, RIM world headquarters. I was surrounded by an unruly cluster of squat buildings, none more than eight stories tall. The buildings all looked pretty much the same, with no hint as to which contained the executive offices. I tried one. Wrong. I hopped back in my car and drove to another. Eventually, I found the right one.

As I was ushered in, I looked around, expecting to see the usual trappings of a tech-firm head office. There was the usual high-tech corporate security. But beyond that, there was no fancy, avant-garde furniture, little in the way of art, no design flourishes, and certainly no foosball tables. The conference rooms, functional but not ornate, were named after legendary Canadian hockey players such as Wayne Gretzky and Gordie Howe. Walking around, you might guess you were in the regional office of a prosperous but unexceptional Canadian company, rather than in the global head-quarters of one of the world's most innovative enterprises.

It's not that the folks at RIM don't care about design. As mak-ers of the ubiquitous BlackBerry, they've built a company with a market value of as much as $84 billion on the design, manufac-ture, and marketing of wireless communications devices. But for them, design isn't a cooler-than-thou office compound with beanbag chairs and cerulean walls. Design isn't just about making things beautiful; it's also about making things work beautifully. Design is about moving knowledge along the funnel, starting from the mystery of how to enable and enhance communication in a mobile age. At RIM, design is about design thinking.

## Leading Design

As I was soon to discover, RIM is headed by one of the most committed and remarkable design thinkers—Mike Lazaridis, RIM's founder, president, co-CEO, and design visionary. Lazaridis is responsible for product strategy, R&D, product development, and manufacturing. His co-CEO, Jim Balsillie, leads the business side of RIM, including corporate strategy, sales, and finance. It's a uniquely successful partnership between two starkly different men. Balsillie is a sleek bundle of contained energy, his quick mind—and mouth—racing from one idea to the next. Next to the angular, athletic Balsillie, Lazaridis cuts a softer, heavier figure, with a thick mane of prematurely grey hair. He is quietly thoughtful until it comes time to talk about his products. Then, the enthusiasm virtually bubbles out of him. When he shares new products with his board of directors (of which I'm one), he can only be described as wildly excited, genuinely thrilled to share his innovations and to see the reactions. Clearly, designing BlackBerrys makes him happy.

Born in Turkey to Greek parents, Lazaridis was five years old and already fascinated by technology when he immigrated with his family to Canada in 1966. By 1984, Lazaridis was an electrical engineering student at the University of Waterloo, just a few credits shy of graduating. But his real passion was designing gadgets. He convinced his parents to lend him seed money to start a technology company and finally dropped out of the university when the fledgling start-up secured a contract with General Motors.

Lazaridis started out making circuit boards and before long was generating more than $1 million in annual sales. One of his customers was Balsillie, who eventually left his job to help

Lazaridis grow RIM into something even bigger. Lazaridis turned his attention to mobile communication devices. He'd learned about digital signal processing at the university, and combined with the expertise in surface-mount technology he'd gained from his circuit-board work, Lazaridis was convinced he could change the wireless communication marketplace, then entirely dominated by analog technology.

He knew it was a ridiculously lofty goal. All the phone companies were massively invested in analog, while digital was in its infancy. Looking back, he says, "Digital had nothing going for it. It was complicated, it was expensive, it was bulky. Anyone who didn't understand the future, and couldn't see where digital signal processing was going to take us, thought this was ridiculous." His prototype digital devices, he says, could be summed up quickly and derisively: "Three boards, packed with parts, battery lasts maybe fifteen minutes. What the hell is this crap?"[1]

Yet Lazaridis was convinced digital processing was the future, and that RIM could take the lead if it thought about innovation in a way that none of its peers did. It's a philosophy that he maintains to this day. Product design, he says, "has to push the envelope to the point where it seems like you're making a mistake." He argues that you have to strive to make a leap far beyond what is possible at the moment. "It has to be audacious from a technical point of view," he says. "When a little company in Canada decides to build a cellular radio and to build it better than the people who birthed cellular radio—notably Motorola and Ericsson at the time—that's a big, audacious goal."

All the more reason to pursue it, figured Lazaridis and Balsillie. RIM entered the product market with an interactive two-way pager, but Lazaridis already believed that the growth of e-mail would make paging obsolete. He wanted to combine the flexibility of the wireless network with the relatively data-rich communication of e-mail, taking wireless communication beyond the character limits of text messaging. Making a logical leap to what might be, he hit on the idea of a personal digital assistant that would handle e-mail on the go. RIM's signature product, the BlackBerry, was born.

From its inception in 1984 to the launch of the BlackBerry in February 1999, RIM grew relatively slowly. Since the BlackBerry launch, RIM has grown explosively from zero subscribers and $50 million in revenue from its legacy pager products to more than 25 million customers and $11 billion in revenue by February 2009.[2] And the BlackBerry has become an indispensable aid to millions of people. Not for nothing is it nicknamed the CrackBerry.

RIM took its first big mystery—how to provide wireless e-mail to corporate users—and drove it to a heuristic—the first primitive BlackBerry. RIM then drove that heuristic to an algorithm, serving corporate customers around the world through its carrier partners and its own proprietary network. It achieved massive scale and efficiency as it drove through the knowledge funnel. But it didn't stop there.

Lazaridis, who shifted from circuit boards to pagers to Black-Berrys, continually reexamined the original mystery and sought out new mysteries as well. "In a business," he says, "no matter how good the process is, no matter how much you've got it down pat, no matter how much money you're making, how efficient, you have to always go back and say 'Is there something fundamentally wrong with the way we're seeing the market? Are we dealing with incomplete information?' Because that's what's going to get you: it's not necessarily that some young whippersnapper's going to come up with some better idea than you. They're going to start from a different premise and they're going to come to a different conclusion that makes you irrelevant." By watching his competitors, Lazaridis had learned the danger of resting comfortably on existing heuristics and algorithms. "Motorola lost because it didn't embrace the future," he says. "It was too damn good at what it was doing." Seduced by reliability, Motorola had stopped thinking like a designer.

## What Is Design Thinking Anyway?

Design thinking, as a concept, has been slowly evolving and coalescing over the past decade. One popular definition is that design thinking means thinking as a designer would, which is about as circular as a definition can be. More concretely, Tim Brown of IDEO has written that design thinking is "a discipline that uses the designer's sensibility and methods to match people's needs with what is technologically feasible and what a viable business strategy can convert into customer value and market opportunity."[3] A person or organization instilled with that discipline is constantly seeking a fruitful balance between reliability and validity, between art and science, between intuition and analytics, and between exploration and exploitation. The design-thinking organization applies the designer's most crucial tool to the problems of business. That tool is *abductive reasoning*.

Don't feel bad if you're not familiar with the term. Formal logic isn't systematically taught in our North American educational system, except to students of philosophy or the history of science.

The vast majority of students are exposed to formal logic only by inference and then only to the two dominant forms of logic—deductive reasoning and inductive reasoning. Those two modes, grounded in the scientific tradition, allow the speaker to declare at the end of the reasoning process that a statement is true or false.

Deductive logic—the logic of what must be—reasons from the general to the specific. If the general rule is that all crows are black, and I see a brown bird, I can declare deductively that this bird is not a crow.

Inductive logic—the logic of what is operative—reasons from the specific to the general. If I study sales per square foot across a thousand stores and find a pattern that suggests stores in small towns generate significantly higher sales per square foot than stores in cities, I can inductively declare that small towns are my more valuable market.

Deduction and induction are reasoning tools of immense power. As knowledge has advanced, our civilization has accumulated more deductive rules from which to reason. In field after field, we stand on the shoulders of the giants who have come before us. And advances in statistical methods have furnished us with ever more powerful tools for reasoning inductively. Thirty years ago, few in a boardroom would have dared to cite the $R^2$ of regression analysis, but now the statistical tools behind this form of induction are relatively common in business settings. So it is no wonder that deduction and induction hold privileged places in the classroom and, inevitably, the boardroom as the preeminent tools for making an argument and proving a case.

Yet a reasoning toolbox that holds only deduction and induction is incomplete. Toward the end of the nineteenth century, American philosophers such as William James and John Dewey began to explore the limits of formal declarative logic—that is, inductive and deductive reasoning. They were less interested in how one declares a statement true or false than in the process by which we come to know and understand. To them, the acquisition of knowledge was not an abstract, purely conceptual exercise, but one involving interaction with and inquiry into the world around them. Understanding did not entail progress toward an absolute truth but rather an evolving interaction with a context or environment.

James, Dewey, and their circle became known as the American pragmatist philosophers, so called because they argued that one could gain understanding only through one's own experiences. Among these early pragmatists, perhaps the greatest of them and certainly the most intriguing was Charles Sanders Peirce. Peirce (rhymes with "terse") was fascinated by the origins of new ideas and came to believe that they did not emerge from the conventional forms of declarative logic. In fact, he argued that no new idea could be proved deductively or inductively using past data. Moreover, if new ideas were not the product of the two accepted forms of logic, he reasoned, there must be a third fundamental logical mode. New ideas came into being, Peirce posited, by way of "logical leaps of the mind." New ideas arose when a thinker observed data (or even a single data point) that didn't fit with the existing model or models. The thinker sought to make sense of the observation by making what Peirce called an "inference to the best explanation." The true first step of reasoning, he concluded, was not observation but wondering. Peirce named his form of reasoning *abductive logic*. It is not declarative reasoning; its goal is not to declare a conclusion to be true or false. It is modal reasoning; its goal is to posit what could possibly be true. (For further information, see "Why You've Never Heard of Charles Sanders Peirce.")

Whether they realize it or not, designers live in Peirce's world of abduction; they actively look for new data points, challenge accepted explanations, and infer possible new worlds. By doing so, they scare the hell out of a lot of businesspeople. For a middle manager forced to deal with flighty, exuberant "creative types," who seem to regard prevailing wisdom as a mere trifle and deadlines as an inconvenience, the admonition to "be like a designer" is tantamount to saying "be less productive, less efficient, more subversive, and more flaky"—not an attractive proposition. And it is a fair critique that abduction can lead to poor results; unproved inferences might lead to success in time, but then again, they might not.

Some abductive thinkers fail to heed Brown's requirement that the design must be matched to what is technologically feasible, launching products that do not yet have supporting technology. Consider the software designers who inferred from the growth of the Internet that consumers would want to do all their shopping online, from pet supplies to toys to groceries. Online security and back-end infrastructure had not yet caught up to their ideas, dooming them to failure.

Other abductive thinkers fail to address Brown's second requirement: that the innovation must make business sense. Looking back on the dot-com crash, Michael Dell, founder of Dell, argues that little has changed. "Still today in our industry, if you go to a trade show, you walk around and you will find a lot of technology for which there is no problem that exists," he says. "It's like,

## Why You've Never Heard
## of Charles Sanders Peirce

### by Jennifer Riel

Bertrand Russell called him "beyond doubt . . . one of the most original minds of the later nineteenth century and certainly the greatest American thinker ever."[4] So why is Charles Sanders Peirce at best an obscure footnote, while other nineteenth-century American philosophers like William James, Ralph Waldo Emerson, and Henry David Thoreau are still widely read today?

Peirce has been characterized as a prickly misanthrope, which may help explain his low profile. He acknowledged it himself, contrasting his own personality with that of his friend William James: "He is so concrete, so living; I a mere table of contents, so abstract, a very snarl of twine."[5] Many intellectuals have had cranky dispositions, yet have gone on to great acclaim. Unfortunately, Peirce compounded his prickly demeanor with a serious transgression of Victorian propriety.

Peirce's father was a well-respected professor of astronomy and mathematics at Harvard. Peirce, on the other hand, struggled to get any academic appointment, due to a somewhat lackadaisical work ethic.

---

'Hey, look at this, we've got a great solution and there is no problem to solve here.' "[6] Think of the Apple Newton, the world's first portable data assistant. Launched in 1993, it utterly flopped. According RIM's Lazaridis, it was a failure of abduction. "It had no future," he argues. "What problem did it solve? What value did it create? It was a research project. What could you do with it that you couldn't do with a laptop? Nothing. And everything you could do with it, you could do better with a laptop." Apple

It took more than fifteen years after his graduation from Harvard to gain a nontenured position as a lecturer in logic at Johns Hopkins University. The appointment would be short-lived. Early in his career, Peirce married Melusina Fay, daughter of a prominent Cambridge family. While still married to Fay, Peirce took up with Juliette Froissey, a young French girl, openly living and traveling with her. When he and Fay were finally divorced a few years later, he married his mistress just six days after the decree. Puritanical Boston society was aghast. He was thereafter fired by Johns Hopkins and largely shunned by the academic community for the rest of his life.

Peirce had transgressed against the strict rules of a highly religious, morally rigid community. His punishment was swift and far-reaching. He was reduced to poverty for the rest of his life, unable to afford heat in winter and subsisting on charity from local merchants and his old friends from Harvard. He lived in enormous pain, as the result of a nerve disorder diagnosed as facial neuralgia. The pain made him more moody and unpleasant still.

For these reasons, we do not have a sustained body of work from which to get a true sense of his contribution to philosophy and logic. Rather than consult a concise set of abridged works, the Peirce scholar must delve into thousands of handwritten, unpublished manuscripts. So, he remains the tormented, secret hero of American philosophy.

Computer (as it was known then) wasn't wrong when it inferred that customers would value a small, portable, digital assistant, but it didn't ultimately deliver a solution that matched the insight.

So the prescription is not to embrace abduction to the exclusion of deduction and induction, nor is it to bet the farm on loose abductive inferences. Rather, it is to strive for balance. Proponents of design thinking in business recognize that abduction is almost entirely marginalized in the modern corporation and take it upon themselves to make their companies hospitable to it. They choose to embrace a form of logic that doesn't generate proof and operates in the realm of what might be—a realm beyond the reach of data from the past.

That's a risk many leaders won't take. Making Peirce's logical leaps is not consistent or reliable; nor does it faithfully adhere to predetermined budgets. But the far greater risk is to maintain an environment hostile to abductive reasoning, the proverbial lifeblood of design thinkers and the design of business. Without the logic of what might be, a corporation can only refine its current heuristic or algorithm, leaving it at the mercy of competitors that look upstream to find a more powerful route out of the mystery or a clever new way to drive the prevailing heuristic to algorithm. Embracing abduction as the coequal of deduction and induction is in the interest of every corporation that wants to prosper from design thinking, and every person who wants to be a design thinker.

## Solving the Paradox at RIM

Thinking abductively to dive into a mystery is part of the culture at RIM, though Lazaridis uses different language to describe it. Rather than mystery, he prefers the term *paradox*. "It's this whole idea of solving the paradox," he says. "How do you solve a paradox? Well, you have to know what the paradox is." In order to advance knowledge, the design thinker has to get comfortable delving into the mystery, trying to see new things or to see things in a new way.

In the early days of the BlackBerry, Lazaridis saw that laptop users were demanding smaller and smaller devices, while the industry was bumping up against the size limitations of small keyboards and display screens. A standard QWERTY keyboard can only get so small before it becomes awkward and uncomfortable to use. A screen displaying all the information a user expects can be reduced only so much before it becomes unreadable or painfully cluttered.

Staring at this paradox—this mystery—Lazaridis stepped back and asked what could be true. What if users didn't use all their fingers to type? What if the information we think *must* be displayed actually gets in the way of understanding? How could reducing size create a better and more usable product? He worked through the paradox. "When is a small keyboard better?" he asked. "When you can use your thumbs. When is a small display better? When it draws your attention to something important." By moving to a handheld device with a thumb-operated keyboard, RIM changed the game on size. By thinking very carefully about what information actually is essential to the end user, RIM reframed the user interface to be simple and clean.

RIM thought about what could make its device truly delightful to the customer. When it came to e-mail, that meant making sure that the device alerted the user that a new e-mail had arrived only when the message was ready to be displayed: "It's fundamental, but every developer we've ever hired to do this project or rewrite the code makes the same mistake," Lazaridis explains. "They signal you as soon as the e-mail arrives." In that case, the user would be prompted by a buzz, pull out her BlackBerry, and have to wait several seconds for the message to be displayed on the screen. Instead, Lazardis insisted that the message pop onto the screen the moment the device is removed from its holster. "Why should you sit there and wait?" he asked.

Delighting the customer also meant thinking about what the device was really meant to do. Looking back, Lazaridis notes that the BlackBerry's key value wasn't in receiving and sending e-mail. Rather, it was in quickly giving users enough information to decide if they needed more. So RIM designed the display screen on the BlackBerry to give users just enough information to make that determination. When a message arrives on your BlackBerry, he says, "There's a dividing line. You know who it's from, you know the title, and you know a little bit about the message. Everything else is above and below. What we're trying to say is, 'This is what you need to know, without touching anything.' You need to know who it's from, what's the subject, and a little bit of the text to decide if you want to keep reading it or put it away. The value is that it gives you the information you need to decide whether you need to respond or whether you don't need to deal with it right now."

Notifying the user only when the message is ready to be displayed, combined with giving just enough information to allow the user to make a quick assessment of what to do with it, is the BlackBerry breakthrough. "We understood that value," Lazaridis says, "and then everything we did was about that—immediate delivery, the quick keyboard response, all the shortcuts. Making that loop so tight and so easy to form muscle memory around, that's what made it addictive. We worked on that loop and everything else was irrelevant. The browser, who cared? Everyone else was working on how do we put paging systems into this, how do we come up with messaging services so we can charge them and send them alerts and all this. We didn't care. All we wanted to do was get you enough of the e-mail that you could respond. That's all that mattered."

Later on, during RIM's high-growth phase, Lazaridis continued to display the attributes of the design thinker, including a willingness to explore new questions for which there is no time-tested solution. Originally, the BlackBerry was an e-mail device with no voice capability. It was so popular that RIM could have successfully exploited that one product for years. Demand was growing by leaps and bounds in RIM's original market, as corporate IT departments bought BlackBerrys by the bushel for company executives. RIM knew exactly what and how to sell to them. But rather than rest on his laurels, Lazaridis looked back along the knowledge funnel to the next mystery and caught a glimpse of what might come next: a handheld device that merged voice and data.

Consider, too, the evolution in RIM's definition of its core business. Initially, RIM sold its BlackBerrys with a package of minutes of data usage. But eventually, Lazardis and Balsillie realized RIM's strengths lay in designing, building, and marketing communications devices for busy people, not in selling minutes, which was the expertise of wireless carriers such as Verizon and Vodafone. Lazaridis and Balsillie redesigned the distribution model to treat carriers as partners rather than competitors, which in turn opened a powerful new distribution channel for RIM's products.

More recently, Lazaridis wanted to extend the BlackBerry to a rich new market: consumers. He foresaw a day when a competitor in "smart" phones (phones with voice, e-mail, and Web-surfing capability) for the consumer market would gain enough scale to tackle RIM in the corporate market. To head off that unknown rival, Lazaridis went to work creating a new suite of consumer-friendly products (smaller, with a camera and music-handling capabilities). He asked his staff to build the best and smallest Black-Berry they could imagine; he said to his staff, "Define for me what the ultimate BlackBerry is."[7] They came back with smaller and smarter consumer-friendly designs. Soon, these models, the Pearl and the Curve, became RIM's biggest-selling products.

Just as important, the Pearl and the Curve hit the U.S. consumer smart-phone market ahead of Apple's iPhone, establishing a leading market share for the BlackBerry. So rather than having that market to itself, Apple has had to battle with an established consumer player, RIM. Interestingly, RIM's other competitors have had less success in the move to smart phones. "Apple realized the same thing we knew about Nokia and Motorola and all the others, which is that they were too successful and focused on feature phones (without e-mail and Web capability). They weren't betting on the future," says Lazaridis. "They were betting on their engine—their low-cost, high-volume, global supply chain juggernaut. They were missing the point. There will be no feature phones in the future. It will all be smart phones."

Long before the iPhone was even a rumor, Lazaridis was back to work creating the 3G Bold with a dramatically enhanced screen and the media-handling capabilities of an iPod. Next came the touch-screen Storm. Lazaridis recognized that a set of his customers wanted a touch-screen device, but felt that existing touch-screen technology lacked an essential element of the BlackBerry experience—the ability to separate navigation (scrolling to the desired message) from confirmation (opening the message).

Lazaridis again applied abductive logic, driving for a breakthrough technology that allowed the user to separate navigating from confirming on a touch screen while simultaneously providing the positive feedback of a click—the distinctive feature of the Storm.

What makes RIM exceptional is that its leaders make a conscious and overt effort to rebalance the organization against the natural tilt toward reliability, actively pushing knowledge down the funnel. Most businesses stress the overriding importance of continuity and consistency. A concerted effort to balance reliability with validity can appear to threaten those values. But RIM's success demonstrates how validity need not undermine reliability. By embracing both design thinking and abductive thinking, RIM amplifies and extends the strength of reliability, creating a competitive advantage far greater and more lasting than validity or reliability alone. It is both more innovative *and* more efficient than its competitors. Its competitive advantage isn't based on cost leadership or differentiation or a particular resource. The basis of advantage is its speed of movement through the knowledge funnel, which produces perpetual advantage in both cost and innovation.

To understand the source of its advantage, we have to look at the cost dynamics of activities as they move through the knowledge funnel from mystery to heuristic to algorithm. The dynamics can be summarized as an axiom: as knowledge moves through the funnel, costs fall.

## Navigating the Knowledge Funnel

Delving into mysteries is the most expensive activity along the knowledge funnel, because you literally don't know what you are doing. The high cost helps explain why so much research into mysteries is conducted in universities, government-funded labs, and other not-for-profit entities. Research professors spend their entire careers staring into the mysteries of their particular field. Most of their work is not economically viable. It doesn't conform to any particular schedule, budget cycle, or planning document.

When first encountering a mystery, design thinkers have to look at everything, because they don't yet know what to leave out. The danger is that what's omitted might be the key to the mystery. With little to go on, the design thinker employs abductive reasoning to discern a pattern in what to others is still an amorphous whole. Of course, the search for patterns is typically marked by repeated false starts and blind alleys; many abductive inferences to the best expla-nation will be wrong. But with experience, design thinkers learn to spot handholds where others see only a sheer cliff face.

Mysteries, then, are expensive, time consuming, and risky; they are worth tackling only because of the potential benefits of discovering a path out of the mystery to a revenue-generating heuristic. The benefits of moving knowledge to the heuristic stage derive from the process of omission. Instead of having to consider every facet of a mystery, the creator of a heuristic need consider only a subset, which yields results more quickly.

But a heuristic takes advanced skill and judgment to operate. The operators of the heuristic form a cognitive elite in their organization, highly valued for their skill, training, and experi-ence in applying the heuristic. But the organization pays a high cost for their elite capabilities. Driving down those costs provides the motivation for applying abductive reasoning once again, toward moving knowledge to the next stage—the algorithm.

The algorithm generates savings by turning judgment—a general way of getting toward the desired solution—into a formula or a set of rules that, if followed, will produce the desired solution. Having removed further variables and variation from the equation, an algorithm is even more efficient than a heuristic. Algorithms can be run by less experienced and less expensive personnel than can heuristics.

Computer code—the digital end point of the algorithm stage—is the most efficient expression of an algorithm. The unit cost of data entry by a modestly trained clerk in Bangalore is already low, but the cost of a computer to scan an invoice and enter the data into the appropriate cells on a spreadsheet is essentially zero. All that's needed is for someone to operate and monitor the computer. At the code stage, knowledge has been narrowed to the extreme. But with it comes lightning speed and infinitesimal costs, the ultimate efficiency. Code takes the cost dynamic of knowledge to its logical limit.

The analysis of cost dynamics seems to imply that the most profitable course for any company that solves a mystery is to drive it to a heuristic and then to an algorithm so tight it turns to code. Then it should give up on design thinking and run that code forever, making heaps of money for shareholders. But that approach is shortsighted, because, as I discussed in chapter 1, it fails to capitalize on the option that the company created—at sizable human and economic cost—as it pushed knowledge quickly through the knowledge funnel. To exploit that opportunity, a company can choose to redeploy its design thinkers. By putting them to work on new mysteries, the company both defends its current position and goes on the offensive, like RIM's Lazaridis, who has continually reinvented both products and strategy by tackling new mysteries and revisiting heuristics and algorithms that grew out of answers to older mysteries.

## Roadblocks en Route to Design Thinking

To be sure, there are impediments to effectively ingraining design thinking in an organization. The main roadblock is the corporate tendency to settle at the current stage in the knowledge funnel. Companies often let mysteries remain mysteries, declaring them unsolvable. A studio executive might insist that it's impossible to forecast which movies will hit it big and which will go straight to DVD. A consumer-products executive might declare that it's impossible to accurately predict consumers' changing tastes or how they will react to a price increase. Instead of delving into the mystery, they just create coping mechanisms. The current fad for "emergent strategy" is one mechanism, being nothing more than a clever way to blame a confusing environment for a company's inability to plan ahead. Companies that leave important mysteries as mysteries not surprisingly find themselves with no resources available to solve mysteries, precisely because the companies are so very inefficient.

Another costly impediment to design thinking is the widespread corporate tendency to leave heuristics in the hands of highly paid executives or specialists with knowledge, turf, and paychecks to defend. If they were to advance the heuristic in their heads to the algorithm stage, the company could break the specialist's information monopoly and hand the job to a less costly employee. To them, design thinking might well be seen as a threat to be beaten back.

Another common corporate error is to settle at the algorithm stage without refining that algorithm to code. Some algorithms sit unrecognized and unexploited because they're run by people, not computers. For example, the duties of a manager of a retail store might include preparing the weekly staffing schedule. Making up the schedule entails following strict rules involving a handful of variables and little or no individual judgment. A piece of software could do the job just as well or even better, a fact recognized by such companies as Workbrain and Blue Cube, which automate scheduling for retailers. There are plenty of other recent examples of clerical algorithms being pushed to code and saving incalculable person–hours of mindless work. But the impetus for that work is coming from the supply side, from outside software vendors who perceive what their clients do not: they're using costly labor to run algorithms that could easily be pushed to code.

By clinging stubbornly to one stage of the knowledge funnel, companies squander opportunities to become more efficient in delivering what they are currently delivering. And the overriding emphasis on a single stage crowds out the time and energy needed to explore new mysteries and fashion new heuristics. This sedulous and usually unexamined loyalty to the status quo undercuts the company's best efforts at innovation.

The design–thinking organization, in contrast, reaps the benefit of efficiency as it pushes activities through the knowledge funnel and frees up time and capital to tackle the next knowledge-advancement challenge. But it takes special leadership to stare down the capital markets and do what is necessary to promote the company's long–term health and vibrancy. Chapter 4 explains how, as chairman and CEO of Procter & Gamble, A. G. Lafley managed to convert a tradition-bound, publicly traded company into a design-thinking organization, driven to push knowledge as far and fast as possible, and how he won over a skeptical analyst community in the process. Chapter 5 highlights the way in which an organization's structure, processes, and norms can help or hinder design thinking. Chapter 6 discusses the ways in which leaders can act as guardians of validity to protect their companies against the tendency to let knowledge settle at its current stage.

## CHAPTER 4

# Transforming
# the Corporation

*The Design of Procter & Gamble*

PROCTER & GAMBLE (P&G), the world's largest consumer packaged-goods company, spent most of the 1990s in a restructuring mode. It actively acquired new businesses, diligently pursued cost-cutting measures, and reorganized its business around products rather than geography. It bought and sold businesses, closed plants, and shuttled executives to new positions in the company. By January 1999, it had a new CEO in place and was ready for the challenges of the new century. Or so it seemed.

Instead, by spring 2000, P&G was facing perhaps the greatest crisis in its 165-year history. CEO Durk Jager had spent several months embroiled in a complex but ill-fated potential merger with drug companies Warner-Lambert and American Home Products (now Wyeth). A friendly takeover offer for Gillette was quickly rebuffed. In March, with its core business in decline and acquisitions slowing down, P&G was forced to warn investors that it would suffer its first quarterly profit decline in eight years. In response, the stock, which had already fallen from a cyclical peak of $116 in January to $86, fell by 30 percent, to less than $60 a share, in a single day.[1]

The headlines in the business press that spring told the story: "Procter and Gamble Awash in a Sea of Selling,"[2] "Trouble in Brand City,"[3] "Investors Agonize over P&G Stock Slip; Analysts: Recovery Could Take 3 Years."[4] Investors—and employees—had good reason for their loss of confidence. Revenue growth at the $40 billion company had slowed to a measly 3 percent to 4 percent a year, profit had stagnated, and seven of ten of P&G's biggest billion-dollar brands were losing market share.

Worse, the decline was accelerating. By June, P&G's fiscal year-end was looming and so was yet another profit warning. The company's performance was deteriorating so quickly that the dramatically scaled-back targets set just three months earlier were already far out of reach. Wall Street had long set its watch by P&G's earnings; suddenly, analysts could no longer rely on the company's forecasts, and the Street took its frustrations out on P&G's stock. P&G shares stalled around $60; analysts scorched management in their reports and downgraded their recommendations. P&G, they said, was no longer a sure bet for long-term growth.

P&G's board had seen enough. For the first time in the company's storied history, directors fired the chairman and CEO. As they considered Jager's successor, directors saw one obvious candidate: A. G. Lafley, who had recently returned from a successful assignment running the Asia-Pacific business to head both the North American region and the global beauty business. Directors worried that Lafley, then fifty-three, needed several years more seasoning. But P&G was a promote-from-within company; there were no other compelling internal candidates, and it would be almost unthinkable to bring in an outsider, no matter how deep the crisis. So, on June 8, 2000, the board appointed Lafley as CEO. To ease their concerns about Lafley's relative youth and inexperience, directors asked Jager's predecessor, the capable and popular John Pepper, to come out of retirement and serve as chairman for Lafley's first two years. The headline in P&G's hometown paper, the *Cincinnati Enquirer*, read, "Bruised P&G Turns to New, Old Leaders."

Investors remained wary. P&G stock fell $4 to $57.50 on the day Lafley's promotion was announced and fell below $55 by the end of June. In less than six months, P&G had dropped from the twenty-first largest company in the world, as measured by market capitalization, to fifty-first, just over one-third the value of Walmart, its biggest customer.[5]

Shareholders, analysts, employees, and retail customers were unhappy, and they were all looking expectantly at Lafley. He recognized that at the heart of their discontent lay a single, disturbing trend: P&G's value equation—the value P&G created for consumers relative to the cost of creating that value—was becoming increasingly unfavorable. The company was introducing fewer and fewer successful new products and brand extensions, and was taking longer and longer between introductions. Meanwhile, P&G's costs, especially in research and development—were soaring. P&G's faltering pace gave Lafley's immediate customers—big global retailers like Walmart and Tesco—an opening, which they were quick to seize. They aggressively courted shoppers with their own in-house, private-label products, hoping to persuade them to switch from P&G's more expensive, branded offerings. The push was successful; as Lafley studied the competition reports, he could plainly see that private-label brands were taking market share from P&G in many categories.

Lafley knew there was only one way to win back straying shoppers and convince others not to leave the reservation: P&G had to become more innovative, so that customers would be willing to pay a premium for P&G products. But innovation could not come at any cost. The expense side of the value equation also had to be addressed. P&G needed to become more efficient, so that it could charge a lower premium to customers and still keep shareholders happy with steady growth in profits and margins. There was just one problem: conventional business thinking said that a company could have innovation or it could have efficiency, but not both at once. There was, according to the received wisdom, always a trade-off.

Although he was a rookie CEO, Lafley was prepared to take bold action to pull P&G out of its downward spiral. Design thinking, he believed, offered a way out of the trade-off between innovation and efficiency. He committed to turning P&G into a design organization, beginning with his senior leadership team. In 2001, only a year into his tenure, he appointed Claudia Kotchka as the corporation's first-ever vice president for design strategy and innovation. Her mandate was to build P&G's design capability and act as the corporation's champion of design thinking. (See "Building a Design-Thinking Organization from Within.")

# Building a Design Thinking Organization from Within

### by Jennifer Riel

The first time A. G. Lafley offered Claudia Kotchka the job of heading up P&G's design initiative, she turned him down flat. In fact, when he approached her again a few months later, she turned him down a second time. Kotchka had reason to say no. She had recently launched Tremor, a new word-of-mouth marketing initiative within P&G, and did not feel ready to let it go. And she was wary. She knew that creating a design-thinking organization would be a major effort, and she wondered if the newly minted CEO would have the time to devote to it: "He had a lot on his plate, so I just didn't think this would be a priority. I knew that if it was not a priority for him, it was never going to happen. It was just too big an effort."[6]

But by September 2001, when Lafley came to Kotchka for the third time, she could see that he was truly serious about embedding designing into the DNA of P&G. "I knew he had decided it was critical. The question that I asked him was, 'What's your vision for the company, and how does this fit in?' That was what I needed to know," Kotchka explained. Lafley replied that he planned to leave five legacies by the end of his tenure as CEO. Design was one of them. Kotchka thought, "Okay, if this is one of the five important things for him to leave the company, it's a big enough change that I will absolutely take it on."

Some questioned why Lafley had handpicked Kotchka for the task; she was a proven performer and dynamic internal entrepreneur, but absolutely not a designer in her own right. Lafley wanted Kotchka for the balance she struck between business and design. As he explained to her, "In order to do this, I need someone who can speak both languages—the language of design and the language of business." Lafley understood that credibility with the business folks would be essential, but so would an ability to understand designers, to know what makes them tick and how to apply their skills to business. Kotchka, who was trained as an accountant but who had been drawn to design as she took on corporate marketing roles, was the perfect fit.

Embedding design into a company as big as P&G, and one with such a strong and defined culture, was a massive challenge. "A. G. had always been a believer in design," Kotchka said, "but the company, I would say, had not." Reflecting on her time as P&G's design czar, a role from which she has recently retired, she laid out several key steps needed to bring design into an organization:

### Set expectations clearly up front and get your boss on board

The first thing Kotchka did when she finally accepted the job was to draw up a contract with Lafley, outlining what she could do, what she could not, and what she would need from him to make it happen. The contract, Kotchka said, was invaluable: "Getting very clear with him in what I could accomplish, how long it would take, was probably one of the smartest things I did. We had a very clear plan of what I was going to do and what he was going to do, and that paid dividends later."

In her view, the most important thing to agree on was where to begin. Kotchka was adamant that she needed to start in the areas of the company where there was an existing interest in design thinking, rather than in the areas of greatest need: "I said, 'I'm going to start where there's suction. I can't force design on some business that doesn't want it.'" Lafley ultimately agreed.

Kotchka also got early agreement on the time line. She studied the path that Dutch electronics giant Philips, an acknowledged design leader, had taken to transform itself from a manufacturing company into a consumer-centric design organization, and concluded that it would take P&G about the same amount of time. "It took them ten years, so I told [Lafley] that. I was very clear about the fact that this was the kind of time line we were looking at. He said do it in five," she said with a laugh. "But at least we were clear it wasn't going to happen overnight."

### Get help (you'll need it)

Kotchka turned to outside experts like IDEO, her external design board, and a trio of deans (Roger Martin, Patrick Whitney, and David Kelley) to supplement her own skills and expertise, but she also hired the best design talent she could find. Unfortunately, she needed senior talent, and P&G's recruiting apparatus was set up to hire new graduates straight out of college. "It takes at least ten, maybe fifteen years to really get mastery in design," she said. Kotchka didn't have the time to start from the bottom; she needed to import some expertise. In the end, she broke with P&G custom and used outside recruiters to help find that talent.

### Expect some speed bumps

Well aware of the difficulty of creating a design organization within P&G, Kotchka was nonetheless surprised by some of the challenges that popped up along the way. The corporate culture at P&G was not set up to support design thinking, and she needed to work long and hard to adapt the internal systems to work for her designers. Everything from the recruiting process to the physical work environments to the way in which market research was conducted needed to change in order to allow design to take hold in the organization. "Everything," she said, "was designed against us."

### Don't try to talk about it. Just demonstrate it.

Kotchka found that the importance of design and its transformative effects could not be explained, only experienced. To illustrate her point, she cited market research, a traditional strength of the company, with traditional practices. For years, P&G had sworn by focus groups. Designers, on the other hand, prefer to go deeper than a focus group allows, spending time one on one with users to better understand their needs. To move in that direction, Kotchka had to slowly validate the new approach over the course of a few years. She would send senior executives out with designers to experience firsthand how a designer observes, questions, and probes the hidden dimensions of the user experience. Over time, by seeing up close how design thinking yields new insights, the executives came to embrace it. "Everything we've done has been about demonstrate, demonstrate, demonstrate," Kotchka said, summing up. "They've got to see it; they've got to experience it."

Kotchka set out to build a design function within the organization, assigning designers to sit on the business teams. Her decision to embed designers in the business units was unusual; most other companies centralized the design function. Kotchka felt very strongly that, at P&G, it was essential to have designers sitting inside the core business teams rather than segregated in a central staff function. Her goal for design, she said, was "to really embed it in the culture, not just have a new design function. I needed people in the business units, sitting in the business units every single day, in order to make that happen." Kotchka said that the decision, questioned at the time and utterly unprovable in advance, was one of her most important strategic choices: "They're definitely part of the business team, and that was our goal. We wanted a seat at the table. We wanted design to be sitting on the leadership team, wherever decisions get made, and have a voice. And we wanted the business units to really understand design, participate in design, and not see it as a black box."

To help P&G better understand design, Kotchka also reached outside the organization to build a network of design experts. She created an external design board made up of world-class designers such Tim Brown, CEO of IDEO; John Maeda, president of the Rhode Island School of Design; and Ivy Ross, Gap's executive vice president of marketing. While the board does review P&G's designs, it is also a key sounding board for the business teams. Teams come to the board for help in thinking through intractable problems or for review and critique of preliminary solutions. The external board works, Kotchka said, because members are not pursuing a personal agenda and have no legacy to protect when they turn their minds to P&G's dilemmas. In addition to the design board, Kotchka built close working relationships with several outside design agencies, particularly with David Kelley and Tim Brown of IDEO. In 2003, Lafley took his entire thirty-five-person Global Leadership Team to the IDEO offices in San Francisco for a day and a half of immersion in design thinking that Kotchka said illustrated clearly that "design is not about making things pretty: Lafley's leadership team really got to experience design thinking for the first time."

Experience, Kotchka felt, was the key. Once P&Gers, from the senior team down, got to experience design thinking, they would be converted. The question was how to create an experience that could be accessed by tens of thousands of employees around the world.

## Building Design into the Company's DNA: DesignWorks

Kotchka wanted an intervention that would encourage and facilitate P&G's category leadership teams to really engage in design thinking to solve problems. For help, she turned to three deans: David Kelley of the Hasso Plattner Institute of Design at Stanford (aka the d. school) and also cofounder of IDEO; Patrick Whitney of the Institute of Design at the Illinois Institute of Technology; and me, from my perch at the Rotman School of Management in Toronto.

In 2005, as a group, we began discussions about creating a comprehensive program that would provide practical experience in design thinking to P&G leaders. We believed that design thinking for business broke down into three essential components: (1) deep and holistic user understanding; (2) visualization of new possibilities, prototyping, and refining; and (3) the creation of a new activity system to bring the nascent idea to reality and profitable operation.

In December, six months after we began our discussions, and with the invaluable help of project manager Heather Fraser, we launched a prototype of the program with the P&G global hair-care business in London, England. The prototype, called Design-Works, was itself an exercise in design thinking. We got a raft of feedback from participants, which we then integrated into refined programs for the cosmetics, skin-care, colorants, fabric-care, and home-care units. One of the most important aspects of the experience, Kotchka argued, was that the participants were working with their close colleagues on problems the teams were facing day to day. "The course was really designed for business teams—a whole business team—to get experience using design thinking, working on real problems," she said. "And that is what makes this course so incredibly successful."

The program also had to be scalable and, as Kotchka said, "designed so we could learn it and run it ourselves." The P&G design leadership, including Kotchka and her second-in-command for DesignWorks, Cindy Tripp, were intensively involved in transferring DesignWorks technology to P&G personnel. By the summer of 2007, P&G personnel were leading DesignWorks exercises independently. The program has since extended its tendrils through the organization. Now, not a day goes by without a DesignWorks session taking place somewhere in the P&G universe, led by one of their hundred and fifty or so trained facilitators, not necessarily designers but members of business units who have expressed an interest and volunteered their time. "These things are literally going on every day, and we don't even know where or when," Kotchka noted happily.

DesignWorks began by encouraging category teams to seek a deeper understanding of their consumers, to stare into mysteries and not continue to utilize the same old heuristic. The hair-care category team, for example, went to a styling salon to observe how women actually used styling products, a part of the hair-care category in which P&G is underdeveloped compared with its leadership position in shampoos and conditioners. The next day, the team members brought those customers back to talk about their experience at the salon. Drawing on what they learned from those discussions, the category team explored how to create an at-home user experience that rivaled the salon experience. They created prototypes of the experience, tested them at the salon, one on one with each member of the user group, and incorporated their learning into the next product iteration. Finally, they worked on converting the refined experience into a system of activities that P&G could execute with sustainable advantage over competitors.

The category leadership teams emerged from the process with a greater understanding and appreciation for design thinking. The course both models and teaches the organized pursuit of new knowledge, looking up the knowledge funnel and seeking productive new insights. "The business teams think they're coming to do packaging," Kotchka said with a laugh. She told the story of one finance manager who said that before the program he didn't see the need to learn about package design. "And afterwards, he came to me and said, 'Claudia! This is amazing! I can see how I can use this in my everyday work.' And that is the goal. They all walk out with solutions they would have never thought of before; this is the whole idea behind design thinking. It's going to take you to a place you've never been. And that's what it does every time." While DesignWorks alone does not establish a balance between reliability and validity at P&G, it gives senior managers a set of tools and a process for engaging in validity-oriented thinking in a creative, practical way.

## Designing New Processes

In addition to equipping his managers with more skills and expertise in design thinking, Lafley worked to change organizational norms to support design thinking. He modeled that thinking in his own behavior, doing in-depth at-home visits with consumers wherever he traveled. He even chatted (through a translator) with rural Chinese women washing clothes in a river. After all, they use detergent too.

He changed key processes, including strategy review. The tradition at P&G was that each category president came to the annual review with a thick deck of slides that culminated in a single right answer for the coming year, including all the inductive and deductive proof needed to gain the approval of the CEO and senior management. Additional slides were prepared to address any objections top management could conceivably raise.

Lafley recognized that this process was a recipe for producing reliability, not validity. The category presidents wanted their strategies to be airtight, so risky creative leaps were out of the question. Lafley saw he had to stop the drive for reliability before it gathered momentum, so he devised a new process. Presidents would submit their slide decks two weeks before the strategy review. Lafley would read the materials and issue a short list of questions that he wanted to discuss at the meeting. He emphasized that he wanted a discussion, not a presentation. Presidents were allowed to bring only three more pieces of paper—charts, graphs, notes—to the review. Only by more or less forcing category managers to toss around ideas with senior management, he reasoned, could they become comfortable with the logical leaps of mind needed to generate new ideas.

At first the presidents and their teams bridled at Lafley's new process. Actual dialogue at the senior levels of P&G was exceedingly rare before Lafley became CEO. Rather than engaging in dialogue, executives devoted their time and energy to bulletproofing arguments and then advocating and defending them. Dialogue was different, foreign—and unnerving. Only after two or three cycles did it dawn on the presidents how invigorating and mind opening it was to engage in dialogue about what could be rather than what was. It was also great for their businesses. Freed from the demand to come up with the single right answer and prove it, they started to work out bigger bets with the corporate team.

To elevate design thinking in the corporate hierarchy of values, Lafley made the solving of wicked problems a high-status, glamorous assignment. (For a short primer, see "Wicked Problems.") For instance, the executives who turned around the baby-care business, which had been in secular decline for almost a decade, were at least as highly rewarded as those running bigger or more stable businesses. He also set up explicitly project-based work with managers, making clear that their work was time bound and that they would go on to another project or assignment when they had completed their current project.

In addition to building skills and changing organizational processes and norms, Lafley made dramatic interventions at each stage of P&G's knowledge funnel, converting mysteries to heuristics and heuristics to algorithms during his time as CEO.

### Converting Mysteries to Heuristics

At the mystery end of the funnel, Lafley was frustrated with P&G's success rate for innovation projects. By the time he became CEO, a mere 15 percent of R&D projects were meeting their internal targets. Even though P&G was an acknowledged R&D powerhouse in the consumer packaged-goods sector, with a track record of game-changing innovations like disposable diapers, anti-dandruff shampoo, and fluoride toothpaste, it was not earning the returns on innovation spending needed to maintain a winning value equation.

Lafley recognized that despite P&G's record of innovation and mammoth R&D budget, its R&D organization was not distinctly better than the competition at converting mysteries to heuristics. In fact, engaging with mysteries was not the R&D department's strong suit. Its forte was honing and refining existing discoveries and making sure that the portfolio of existing P&G products kept improving and optimizing in ways that consumers would recognize and value. The original Pampers disposable diaper was a genuine breakthrough, a risky and imaginative solution to the mystery of diaper washing. But once that innovation took hold in the market, P&G's R&D department turned its attention to the steady improvement of the disposable diaper. Software guru Bill Buxton calls this sort of activity N+1 innovation.[7] Lafley was confident that when it came to N+1 innovation, P&G was the best in its competitive space. But N+1 innovation was not going to yank P&G out of the doldrums.

P&G needed true discovery activity: the conversion of mystery to heuristic, which Lafley recognized is widely distributed in the world. Large corporations like P&G do not produce a share of discoveries proportionate to their investment in the pursuit. On the other hand, independent inventors, small invention-focused firms, and academic researchers produce a share of discoveries wildly disproportionate to the resources they apply to the task. They work independently of reliability-oriented organizations that insist they prove every initiative or undertaking with empirical data. Instead, they work in validity-based environments—sometimes

## Wicked Problems

### by Jennifer Riel

Lots of problems are hard: differential calculus, for instance. Or determining the optimal production schedule for a new manufacturing plant. Or assigning a realistic value to stock options. Hard problems are complex and take many steps from beginning to end, making it difficult to see your way clear to the solution from the outset. Hard problems face us at every turn, but fortunately business schools specialize in giving us the analytical tools that allow us to tackle and solve these problems.

So hard problems aren't the problem. The real challenge that faces the CEO and the young manager alike is that not all problems are hard problems. In fact, many of them belong to an entirely different category: wicked problems.

Wicked problems aren't merely harder or more complex than hard problems. They don't just involve more factors or stakeholders. They don't just take us longer to solve. Analytical thinking alone, no matter how skillfully applied, isn't going to generate an answer to a wicked problem.

Wicked problems, first identified by mathematician and planner Horst Rittel in the 1960s, are messy, aggressive, and confounding. Rittel's notion of wicked problems was detailed by C. West Churchman in a 1968 issue of *Management Science*. Churchman described wicked problems as "a class of social system problems which are ill-formulated, where the information is confusing, where there are many clients and decision makers with conflicting values, and where the ramifications in the whole system are thoroughly confusing."[8] In other words, wicked problems are ill-defined and unique in their causes, character, and solution.

Here's how to tell if you have a wicked problem:

- The causes of the problem are not just complex but deeply ambiguous; you can't tell why things are happening the way they are and what causes them to do so.

- The problem doesn't fit neatly into any category you've encountered before; it looks and feels entirely unique, so the problem-solving approaches you've used in the past don't seem to apply.

- Each attempt at devising a solution changes the understanding of the problem; merely attempting to come to a solution changes the problem and how you think about it.

- There is no clear stopping rule; it is difficult to tell when the problem is "solved" and what that solution may look like when you reach it.

It's almost as if attempting to solve a wicked problem is like that old cliché of trying to grasp a handful of sand: the harder you grip, the more sand slips through your fingers. The more you think about the problem, the more wicked it becomes.

With hard problems, your job is to look at the situation, identify a set of definite conditions, and calculate a solution. With wicked problems, the solution can no longer be the only or even the primary focus. Instead, dealing with wicked problems demands that attention be paid to understanding the nature of the problem itself. Problem understanding is central; the solution, secondary. It's no wonder that so many designers have come to embrace the notion that their role is to work with wicked problems. "Designers thrive on problem *setting,* at least as much as problem *solving,*" explains Bill Buxton, principal researcher for Microsoft.[9]

In a world rife with wicked problems—the end of oil, the battle for talent, confounding mysteries of all kinds—the companies that succeed will be those that make a valued place for design thinkers, for those people who thrive on setting and solving wicked problems, throughout their organization.

no more than a basement workbench—that are conducive to producing desired breakthroughs, however inconsistently and infrequently they might emerge.

With so many talented inventors working at discovery, Lafley saw the futility of P&G's insistence that all its product innovation be homegrown. With the help of colleagues in his R&D organization, Lafley championed a wholly new approach to R&D called Connect + Develop. Connect + Develop called for P&G to *connect* with innovators outside the P&G tent and *develop* their creations as only P&G could. He set a goal that P&G would source half its product innovation from outside the company. P&G's contribution would consist of adding value to these inventions by exercising its state-of-the-art capabilities in qualifying inventions, honing and refining them for the market, and distributing the eventual product on a mass scale. When it came to branding, positioning, pricing, and distributing a great new product, P&G's capabilities were unmatched. Not surprisingly for a big corporation, those activities were one or two stages removed from mysteries; commercialization and branding are mainly heuristics, and selling and distribution have largely been refined to algorithms.

In essence, the Connect + Develop initiative, through its networked approach, bulked up P&G's supply of ideas in the mystery-to-heuristic transition where it was thin, enabling it to feed more opportunities into its well-developed heuristics and algorithms, which had idle capacity. By doubling the volume of discoveries entering the funnel, Lafley doubled the capacity of the overall funnel. Among the successful products to emerge from P&G's knowledge funnel since Lafley launched Connect + Develop are the

Crest SpinBrush, the Mr. Clean Magic Eraser, and the Tide to Go stain remover. By 2006, at least 35 percent of P&G's new products had elements that originated outside the company, well on the way to Lafley's goal of 50 percent in five years.

### Driving Heuristics to Algorithms

Like most large corporations, P&G employs an army of highly paid and extremely talented managers who spend their days running the same heuristic processes over and over (though this may come as news to them). In fact, the vast majority of corporate employees earning six figures or more spend most of their time operating a personal heuristic—a high-level intellectual exercise requiring considerable personal judgment, which their organization depends on them to provide. They have no obvious incentive to drive their own heuristic down the knowledge funnel to an algorithm, because an algorithm can be run by a less experienced and dramatically cheaper human resource. Unless given an incentive to free up time to stare into the next mystery, managers valued for their skill at running a heuristic will jealously guard their domain.

Lafley realized that because heuristic skill is so highly rewarded, even some of P&G's most essential and long-running activities—above all, brand building—still existed only as heuristics in the heads of scarce and costly senior executives. Despite its central importance to P&G, very little of the brand-building heuristic had actually been committed to paper. In part, that is because P&G itself isn't a marketplace brand the way Tide, Pampers, and Crest are. Those individual brands are managed by the global category teams that have grown up around them. Those teams have become a magnet for marketers who want to hone their brand-building expertise to the highest possible pitch. Among the alumni of P&G's brand-building academy are Steve Ballmer of Microsoft; Meg Whitman, formerly of eBay; Jeff Immelt of GE; James Hackett of Steelcase; and Scott Cook of Intuit. But because little had been done to shift brand building significantly toward an algorithm, a great deal of knowledge about building brands existed only in the oral history of the company and in the heads of its current brand-building experts. The only way to understand what brand building actually entailed at P&G was to hang around the experts, watching and trying to learn from what they did and said.

With Lafley's support and encouragement, P&G made a conscious, top-down effort to drive the brand-building heuristic toward algorithm. Lafley engaged some of his best brand builders and thinkers to document a brand-building framework and drive it toward an algorithm (recognizing that, because of brand building's complexity and inherent subjectivity, it is unlikely ever to be a true algorithm). Like all good design thinkers, the group put out a first prototype—Brand Building Framework 1.0—and then solicited user feedback, integrating the findings into the next iterations of the model, which became Brand Building Frameworks 2.0, 3.0, and so on. For the first time in P&G history, junior marketers had a detailed, regularly updated process document to use in learning and practicing brand building. The days are gone when all a fledgling marketer could do was watch and listen to the masters, trying to infer what they were up to.

What is most remarkable about the work of writing down P&G's embedded brand-building wisdom is that it had for so long been simultaneously the most important thing at P&G *and* the least documented. One might have imagined that it would be the most documented, but that ignores the powerful incentives that heuristics runners have to keep their heuristics to themselves. P&G is systematically stripping away those incentives in order to drive much of the brand-building discipline all the way to an algorithm.

The Brand Building Framework has two goals. The first is to give junior marketers the tools needed to do much of the work previously done by high-cost elites. But those elites have not been made redundant. By handing over the routine part of their jobs to junior staffers, senior brand builders are free to accomplish the framework's second goal of focusing their considerable talents on the next mystery in order to create the next brand or brand extension that consumers want. Some of these managers may never be comfortable exploring mysteries, but others will be. They are P&G's pioneers, pointing the way to the organization's future as they drive the brand-building heuristic toward an algorithm.

## Design in Unlikely Places

Design thinking can create value in areas of the corporation far removed from marketing and product development. Design thinking, for example, transformed P&G's Global Business Services into a design shop. The effort began in 1998, when P&G undertook its most significant reorganization in more than twenty years. Seven global business units (GBUs) replaced the previous structure, which had divided P&G's businesses into four geographic regions. In the new structure, rather than having four separately managed, regional detergent businesses, P&G would have a single detergent business with profit responsibility for the entire globe.

Second, P&G created five market-development organizations (MDOs) to distribute products in the various markets on behalf of the GBUs. The MDOs were accountable for sales volume but not profits. Third, it created a global shared services organization (Global Business Services or GBS) to deliver employee services, facilities management, financial and accounting reporting, purchasing, and information technology. It was a bold reorganization, in which P&G created the first global market-facing organization (MDO) in its industry and a truly integrated, global shared services organization (GBS).

In 2002, P&G took an even more momentous step with GBS. Realizing it had gone as far internally as it could to drive scale, the leaders of GBS made the strategic decision to outsource key business processes. Rather than outsourcing to one integrated provider, P&G opted to establish relationships with best-of-breed partners that were leaders in their field, including Hewlett-Packard for IT infrastructure and accounts payable, Jones Lang LaSalle for facilities management, and IBM for employee services. More than two thousand GBS employees transferred to the partner firms.

During the decision-making process, Filippo Passerini was a key GBS advocate for the best-of-breed strategy. In 2003, Passerini was named head of GBS. Passerini's challenge was considerable, as was his opportunity. He recognized that GBS had now outsourced the most algorithmic of its activities. Those activities were the most readily translated into service-level agreement terms in outsourcing contracts. The question now was how to think about the GBS services and employees that remained.

Passerini's vision was to redefine GBS as an agile design shop whose employees would focus on opportunities to turn heuristics into algorithms and refine algorithms into code. This meant attacking wicked problems that bedeviled P&G, working on a project basis rather than a permanent basis, and flowing teams of GBS staff to whatever work was deemed most critical and time sensitive.

For example, the product category teams around the world prepared each year for strategy and planning exercises by assembling a binder of information on the overall business environment, competitive challenges, and the like. GBS staffers noticed that the binders contained many common elements and saw an opportunity to streamline the process into an algorithm. A GBS team wrote code that automatically pulled together the vast majority of the information into integrated, online "decision cockpits" that put the information the executives needed at their fingertips. Automating that task freed up the organization for higher-level work.

The flow-to-the-work project culture also helped P&G integrate the $57 billion acquisition of Gillette, itself a global organization with $10 billion in sales and thirty-five thousand employees. GBS, together with its partners, flowed numerous project teams to work on the Gillette integration and completed it flawlessly, a huge undertaking. GBS moved all Gillette's systems, encompassing a corporation operating in more than two hundred countries and territories worldwide, onto P&G's platform. The pressure to work quickly and efficiently was intense: P&G management had publicly projected $1.2 billion in synergy savings. By flowing teams to the work, GBS was able to deliver the systems integration in just fifteen months. It was the largest and fastest integration in P&G's history and took far less time than large-scale integration efforts at other leading corporations.

With the transformation of GBS—and its continued success as a partner to business units in tackling wicked problems—morale has soared. GBS personnel now point with pride to their record of taking over an activity and delivering equal or better service at a substantial reduction in cost. That savings gives P&G the lowest cost of shared services in the industry and puts it on a path to significantly reduce the cost of shared services as a percentage of sales. And it has made Passerini a star among chief technology officers for sowing creativity across traditionally administrative functions such as employee services, facilities management, and IT. Rather than focusing exclusively on honing, refining, and cutting the cost of current algorithms, his organization's focus is on helping P&G speed activities through the knowledge funnel, whether in-house or through an outsourcing partner.

At each stage of P&G's transformation into a design-thinking organization, Lafley aimed at driving activities down the P&G knowledge funnel, shaving costs and gaining speed in the process. Within three years of Lafley's appointment as CEO, P&G was transformed from a mature company with slowing growth, eroding profits, and moribund brands into a genuine growth company, with profit growth of 15 percent per year. Thirteen of its top fifteen brands had increased their market share. Within six years, revenues were $70 billion and growing at a consistent 10 percent clip. P&G's roster of billion-dollar brands expanded to twenty from ten, and several other brands were flirting with that benchmark. R&D spending fell from 4.8 percent of sales to 3.6 percent, yet the success rate of its new-product initiatives had quintupled to 65 percent. Profit had doubled and was growing at 15 percent annually. But perhaps the surest sign that Lafley had won over the reliability-oriented financial community was the growth in P&G's market value. Within three years, it had doubled to nearly $200 billion, making P&G one of the ten most valuable companies in the world, ahead of Johnson & Johnson and about the same as Walmart. No single factor can account for such an impressive and thorough turnaround, but by almost any measure, the P&G of today is dramatically more innovative *and* strikingly more efficient than the P&G of just a few years ago. As an argument for the power of design thinking, that's hard to top.

## CHAPTER 5

# The Balancing Act

*How Design-Thinking Organizations*
*Embrace Reliability and Validity*

IN EARLY 1993, I SPENT the first of many pleasant nights at Marigold Lodge on the north shore of Lake Macatawa, in Holland, Michigan. Macatawa isn't really a lake but a large inlet with a narrow mouth, on the eastern shore of Lake Michigan, about forty-five minutes southwest of Grand Rapids. The inn was at the end of a discreet lane off a long, winding, backwoods road, located on a little peninsula that juts out into the lake. The rooms were small and austere, with no television or other modern conveniences. Dinner in the dining room looking out on the lake was a wonderful experience, but I'd been told not to ask for a glass of wine with my meal—no alcohol was allowed.

The place had a distinguished, elegant feel befitting its 1913 Prairie School origins. But something did feel very modern—the furniture. Every piece was sleek and perfectly suited to its placement and function, from the compact desk in the room to the side tables in the dining room to the undulating molded-wood area dividers, which I later learned are precious, original Eames screens. I shouldn't have been surprised. Since 1978, Marigold Lodge has been owned by Herman Miller, Inc., one of the world's leading office furniture companies, headquartered in nearby Zeeland, Michigan, and has served as its training center and home for visiting designers.

Zeeland and its surrounding area form the heart of Dutch Reform country in western Michigan. Dutch cabinetmakers settled the area, hence the tulip festivals, the replica windmills, and, sadly, the absence of wine at dinner. The cabinetmakers built a leading home-furnishing industry here, and when the industry began to move to the southeastern states in search of lower labor costs, the western Michigan firms migrated successfully toward higher-end office furniture. The area became and remains the home of the global office furniture industry, with giants Steelcase, Herman Miller, and Haworth situated nearby.

The purpose of that first visit in 1993 was to begin work on strategy with the top management team of Herman Miller. The work lasted two years, but it made an impression on me for life. In my previous dozen years as a strategy consultant, I had never encountered a place like Herman Miller. I had worked for giant firms like P&G, AT&T, and Nortel, which were much bigger than Herman Miller, as well as a variety that were smaller. But none had the design approach of Herman Miller.

The relationship started out in a unique way. I was hired by the senior vice president of design, a wonderful man named Rob Harvey. To be hired not by the senior strategy officer or the CEO, but by the senior design officer, was a first. Harvey was a true designer who had planned hospitals before coming to Herman Miller. One day he offered to take me to his home, which he had personally designed. It was, he explained, about ninety minutes north of corporate headquarters. That struck me as odd as I drove north for my first visit to Harvey's home. People endure long commutes for the chance to work in Manhattan or Los Angeles, but don't they come to a place like Zeeland, Michigan, to eliminate that commute? Not if you want to design a house that sits on top of the sand dunes that rise high above the eastern shore of Lake Michigan. At Harvey's home, while watching a sunset that rivaled the best in coastal California, we drained ancient bottles of 1961 Bordeaux that he had bought when he was working as a young man in London thirty years earlier.

When I had gotten to know Harvey well enough to ask him why he was in charge of strategy, he responded matter of factly, "Well, Roger, strategy is a design exercise, isn't it?" Sure enough, everything we did as consultants was scrutinized heavily, with Harvey or some other Herman Miller executive wanting to know, for example, why we had designed the market research this way rather than some other way. No organization before or since had wanted to know in such detail the thinking behind the design of every step. Herman Miller was determined to understand the design of its strategy the way it understood the design of its furniture.

I was extremely fortunate to arrive at Herman Miller not long before the launch of the legendary Aeron chair in 1994, so I saw from inside the lead-up to that epic event and the way in which abductive reasoning and a search for validity drove the process. As was customary for Herman Miller, the Aeron chair project was led by two outside designers, Bill Stumpf (who passed away in 2006) and Don Chadwick. Paradoxically, the firm known worldwide for the design excellence of its furniture uses outside industrial designers for virtually all its major projects. Stumpf and Chadwick had previously collaborated with Herman Miller to design the Equa chair, an ergonomic breakthrough launched in 1984 that *Time* magazine had called the Design of the Decade.[1] Within the subsequent decade, every company in the market had a chair that resembled the Equa (see figure 5-1).

The challenge this time for Stumpf and Chadwick was to start with a clean slate and step back from their own assumptions about

**FIGURE 5-1**

## The Equa chair

Photo courtesy of Herman Miller, Inc.

form and material to design a totally new kind of chair. What do people really need when they sit down to work? That was the wicked problem, and it was one of the oldest. Mies van der Rohe, the brilliant designer from the Bauhaus, famously remarked that it is almost easier to design a skyscraper than a chair. A chair must look good and feel comfortable, of course, but it must also provide ergonomic support and adjust in simple ways for whatever task we take on. It should fit, in every sense of the word.

Before they even drew their first sketches, Stumpf and Chadwick visited many offices and spoke to the people who sat in chairs all day. They learned how complex sitting really is, how many different tasks people perform while they are in their chairs, and how the chairs work for or against them as they move. They observed the subtle signals of discomfort, the shifts of position as sitters grew stiff or the seat got too warm. They drew on their experience in materials and engineering to imagine elegant solutions to problems of weight, shape, and contour. And by reasoning what a chair ideally suited might be, they arrived at the unprecedented Aeron chair.

The Aeron, as *Esquire* magazine noted, looks more the X-ray of a chair than the chair itself.[2] In an era when executives signaled their status by sitting in the largest, most padded, and most luxuriously upholstered chair in the room, Stumpf and Chadwick appeared with a chair that had no padding or upholstery whatsoever (see figure 5-2). In their focus groups, users told them it did not even look like a chair. The feature that startled the focus groups most was the porous, screenlike material called Pellicle that makes up the chair's seat and back. Stumpf and Chadwick had wondered why people would shift and reshift while sitting in even the most ergonomic of conventional chairs.

FIGURE 5-2

## The Aeron chair

Photo courtesy of Herman Miller, Inc.

They conducted studies that pinpointed the problem: conventional upholstery retained too much heat. People shifted because they were seeking a cooler position. Pellicle, which breathed instead of soaking up body heat, solved the problem and gave Aeron its unique transparent look. However, as Malcolm Gladwell recounts in his book *Blink*, the early focus groups were turned off by the odd look of the chair, complaining that it was just plain ugly. Some even asked to see the finished version, the one with upholstery and padding added.[3]

It was a unique experience to be working with senior management when this very mixed customer feedback came back from the field. At most companies, the response would be to either drop the project or significantly rework the product and test it until the consumer feedback improved dramatically. But not at Herman Miller. Market research and focus group data didn't trump the work and judgment of the designers. The designers had done detailed work to study the mysteries of how users interacted with the chair they used all day long. They combined that detailed work with their deep expertise in industrial design to make the logical leap of mind to a new design: a radical idea that could not possibly be proven successful in advance. "It was a matter of deliberate design to create a new signature shape for the Aeron chair," said Stumpf. "Competitive ergonomic chairs had become look-alikes. Differentiation was a huge part of the Aeron design strategy."[4]

That the designers were confident of their own design was no surprise. The surprise was that design chief Rob Harvey, seating division president Andy McGregor, and chief executive officer Kerm Campbell gave a green light to this logical leap of mind in the face of mixed data. And it was a big green light. They didn't dribble the Aeron into the market; they launched it with a flourish.

The decision to launch makes perfect sense in light of a story that Harvey told me. Early in his tenure as senior vice president of design, he took an aging D. J. De Pree through a product review. (De Pree was Herman Miller's legendary first CEO, serving for thirty-nine years before turning the job over to his son Hugh and moving up to chairman, where he served an additional seven years. For more on the De Prees, see "The De Prees of Herman Miller.") During the review, De Pree turned to Harvey and asked whether he had gathered the feedback from the sales force on the

## The De Prees of Herman Miller

It is a wicked problem that has perplexed business leaders for decades: how to connect business and design. In a 1965 speech at the Rochester Institute of Technology, Hugh De Pree, one of a troika of De Prees who presided over Herman Miller for over half a century, described how his family tackled the problem. Their solution transformed Herman Miller from a tiny, failing residential furniture manufacturer to a paragon of American design:

> Design is an integral part of the business. The designer's decisions are as important as those of the sales or production departments. It is his responsibility to recognize needs and solve them in his own way. There is no pressure on the designer to modify design to meet the market. Sales and Manufacturing have a responsibility to feed back to Design information that helps the designers to define the problem.
>
> But the designer decides how to use this information. We decide what we will make. If the designer and management like a solution to a particular problem, it is put into production. There is no attempt to conform to the so-called norms of public taste, nor is there any special faith in the methods used to evaluate the buying public. Our designers must not be hamstrung by management's fear of getting out of step. All that is asked of the designer is a valid solution.[5]

Hugh, like his father D. J. and his brother Max, believed the role of designers was to create those valid solutions. The role of sales and manufacturing was to provide feedback that would help designers define problems. The role of top management was to protect the designers from the rest of the company: "In our company, the designers receive and depend upon feedback from Sales and Manufacturing, but they report only to top management." His philosophy follows from firm principles that Gilbert Rohde brought with him when he was hired as Herman Miller's first designer in 1931: "The designer was to retain absolute control over the production of his creations. The manufacturer would not be allowed to change the mechanics or appearance of a design to the slightest degree." The De Prees knew they had to assert the legitimacy of validity in a reliability-oriented environment. Market research, sales, and manufacturing would tilt toward reliability if given a chance. "Valid design" needed top management to provide the counterweight. Hugh De Pree helped establish the authority of design by defining it:

> Designing, then, is a basic activity. It comes to grips with the very essence of a problem and proceeds to develop a solution organically, from the inside out, as opposed to "styling," which concerns itself largely with the distinctive mode of presentation or with the externals of a given solution. The design activity is based upon an understanding of the intrinsic principle of a given problem and its solution.

De Pree believed that designers think in a fundamentally different way from salespeople or manufacturers. But he hinted that protecting and exalting his designers could be trying at times. "Like it or not," he said, "designers are important; indeed, vitally essential for the success of a business enterprise." That "like it or not" is the tip-off that De Pree was speaking as someone who had had his share of conflicts with his indispensable but demanding designers.

The design-friendly culture that the De Prees championed never did take hold across the American corporate landscape. In that 1965 speech, De Pree offered this scathing assessment: "American industrial programs of planned obsolescence have set up an industrial complex geared to producing waste, and a society trained to accept it." His vision of an industrial landscape littered with drab, uninspiring products foreshadowed the consumer-apocalypse wasteland depicted in Pixar's *Wall-E*.

The De Pree design model worked for Herman Miller, thanks to the commitment of the De Pree family. But I am not sure it is the optimal model for other companies. The top managers of the design-thinking organizations of today and tomorrow do not merely place themselves between designers and line managers. They help line managers become design thinkers. They are pioneering the management discipline of business design.

product design that they had just reviewed. He asked the question rather conspiratorially, as if to suggest that he hoped and expected that Harvey had gotten sales-force feedback. Fortunately, the politically savvy Harvey had already asked some of the old guard about De Pree's predilections and learned that De Pree tested all the new executives with this question. Harvey knew that the right answer was, "No, absolutely not!" De Pree smiled in appreciation. "That is right, Mr. Harvey. You never ask the sales force what they think of a design. Their job is to sell it."[6]

That was the Herman Miller culture, handed down from managerial generation to generation and reflected in its processes. The sales function was responsible for providing feedback on users to inform the designers at the outset of their design process. But after that, the designers design and the salespeople sell. The salespeople don't opine on design, nor does any other function.

The Aeron chair went on to become the most successful chair in the history of the office furniture business and won numerous design awards and a place in the permanent collection of the

Museum of Modern Art in New York. Ironically, the chair that users said didn't look like a chair became the iconic representation of a modern chair, which every new ergonomic chair had to resemble. The logical leaps that Stumpf and Chadwick made were validated, as were the structure, processes, and culture of Herman Miller.

## Making a Home for Design Thinking

Design-thinking organizations remain a small minority in the corporate world, and on the whole, they are relatively small themselves (not Herman Miller, however, which was approaching $1 billion in revenues at the time of the Aeron launch). Generally, the larger the company, the less likely it will be receptive to design thinking. The pressure from stakeholders who value reliability over validity is hard to resist. Bankers want to see budget projections and proof that they will be met, boards reject initiatives that can't be proved from prior experience, and shareholders—egged on by equity analysts—demand that the company meet its profit guidance every quarter without fail. The incentives to favor reliability are omnipresent, while the rewards of seeking validity seem distant and uncertain.

But is reliability all that shareholders, analysts, and boards of directors really want? Not if they want a vibrant, growing company. A vibrant, growing company makes discoveries that help it get into new businesses or markets, or help it stay ahead of competitors; it continually reinvents itself. But the rewards for those validity-oriented actions are not immediate; they come only after the world recognizes the positive outcomes. Some validity-driven initiatives will succeed, but many others will fail, to the dismay of stakeholders anchored to the values of consistency and predictability.

With the punishment for lack of reliability so swift and severe, and with the rewards for adhering to validity so distant and speculative, companies have compelling reasons to slide toward more reliability and less validity. In the short run, rewards flow to companies that run, hone, and refine the same heuristic or algorithm rather than seek to move knowledge through the knowledge funnel. In the long run, though, reliability-focused companies grow stagnant and fall prey to new competitors, despite the benefits of incumbency.

In 1928, the Dow Jones Industrial Average was fixed at thirty companies for the first time. Of those original thirty companies, only three remain in the composite. Of the original *Fortune* 100 companies, published in 1955, only eleven are still on the list. In fact, on both original lists, most of the companies either no longer exist or have become part of other companies. For a particularly stark example, think of the U.S. airline industry. The incumbent airlines—American, Delta, United, Northwest, and Continental—were so busy benchmarking against one another and honing the existing model that an upstart airline was able to reconfigure the industry by reimagining the entire flying experience. It cast aside the hub-and-spoke route system in favor of point-to-point direct flights and wooed travel-battered fliers with low prices, direct booking, and friendly staff. That upstart was Southwest Airlines, and today it flies more passengers per year than any other American airline. Before the recession hit in the first quarter of 2009, it had reported seventy consecutive profitable quarters, more than seventeen years of positive performance. The legacy airlines have not fared as well, to say the least.

The bias toward reliability infects even corporate R&D departments, which you might think would be havens for design thinkers. But in cultures where status and rewards flow to reliability's champions and the exploration of mysteries is frowned on, R&D departments tilt toward the "D" part of their mandate and skimp on the "R." The great coup of P&G's Connect + Develop initiative was to exploit that natural inclination in order to beef up its design-thinking capacity. Connect + Develop aggressively sought outside research and fed it into P&G's finely honed development machine, which had the capacity to handle far more research than P&G alone could supply.

While P&G was adding capacity in validity-oriented pursuits, it continued to invest in reliability to achieve and sustain scale. Validity-focused companies, such as design firms, rarely achieve substantial size. The largest industrial design firms in America—IDEO, Design Continuum, and Ziba Design—all command $100 million or less in annual revenue, three orders of magnitude smaller than the largest American industrial firms. Few large companies have managed—or even attempted—to balance sufficient predictability and stability to *support* growth with sufficient creation of new knowledge to *stimulate* growth. Those that do will be the enduring organizations of the future. And as they grow, they will have to think carefully about ways to reinforce design thinking in their own structures and processes. Without careful attention to its organizational structures over time, even the most design-friendly organization will find itself tilting back toward reliability.

To create an environment that balances reliability and validity, that both drives across the stages of the knowledge funnel and hones and refines within stages, a business needs to think differently about three elements of its organization: its structures, its processes, and its cultural norms.

## A Project-Oriented Structure

In the main, companies organize work around permanent jobs and ongoing tasks. "Vice president of marketing" denotes a permanent position with a set of ongoing tasks, such as managing the annual advertising plan, setting marketing budgets, coordinating with sales, and reporting quarterly on share trends to the CEO. This definition of work is entirely suited to a company devoted to running heuristics and algorithms. The work never comes to a terminus. Hotshot corporate lawyers learn and run a particular heuristic for their entire careers. Employees in the accounts payable department come to work every day and run a work-flow algorithm whose essential elements have not changed in fifty years—except that now the algorithm is run at an outsourcing firm in Chennai, India.

In companies organized around ongoing, permanent tasks, roles are rigidly defined, with clear responsibilities and economic incentives linked tightly to those individual responsibilities. This structure discourages all but senior staff from seeing the big picture. People define their work as "my responsibilities," not "our responsibilities." They limit their focus to those individual responsibilities, refining and honing outputs before sharing a complete, final product with others. The senior vice president of marketing will refine and adjust the annual marketing plan until it is airtight. Only then is it presented to the CEO, who, it is hoped, will pronounce it perfect.

As well-suited as that construct is for running known heuristics and algorithms, it is not an effective way to move along the knowledge funnel. That activity is by definition a project; it is a finite effort to move something from mystery to heuristic or from heuristic to algorithm. And such projects demand a business organized accordingly, with ad hoc teams and clearly delimited goals. A design-thinking organization would function more like P&G's Global Business Services (GBS) unit, which uses a fluid, project-based activity system to tackle large undertakings such as the Gillette integration. When the project is finished, the team disbands, reforming in a different configuration suited to the next task at hand. "Flow to the work" is what GBS has come to call its structural approach, and over time, the GBS employees have become increasingly at ease with organizing themselves by projects rather than permanent structures.

Design consultancies illustrate the power of an alternative job structure. Designers are accustomed to being assigned a clearly defined project that comes to an end at a specified date. Designers get used to mixing and matching with other designers on ad hoc teams created with a specific purpose in mind. The typical designer's résumé consists of an accumulation of projects, rather than an accumulation of hierarchical job titles. The project-based approach informs the entire mind-set of the designer. David

Kelley of IDEO illustrates the approach perfectly: "I look forward to going to the IDEO café at breakfast time or talking with my students in the d.school," he says. "I ask the first person I see, 'What are you working on?' "[7] He does so because that person's daily work is defined by project, not title.

The designer's résumé may well reflect reality better than one organized as a progression of titles. Most of work life is a set of projects, each with its own ebbs and flows. Many managers complain that, because they are constantly running around putting out brushfires, they can never focus on their so-called real jobs. But perhaps their real job *is* firefighting projects.

The project-based work style emphasizes collaboration. Projects are typically assigned to teams rather than to individuals, although that team may have its own internal, and often temporary, hierarchy—a captain or a quarterback, as well as linemen to handle the blocking and tackling. But the solution is expected to come from the team, not the quarterback. And the team is expected to include the client in the collaborative process. Rather than waiting until the outcome is just right, the client is exposed to a succession of prototypes that grow more right and more elegant with every iteration.

Architect Frank Gehry is famous for this iterative style. The first design he presents typically provokes a firestorm of protests for its inadequacies. Gehry's initial design for the Art Gallery of Ontario (AGO) elicited an apoplectic reaction from one of the gallery's most important benefactors. Thinking the design slighted the part of the gallery he considered his baby, he resigned from the board, swearing off any further involvement with the institution. But Gehry was at the beginning of his process, not the end point. He wanted feedback that he could incorporate into his next iteration, which would not be final either. The final design was still many iterations away.

Many corporate managers who engage designers could sympathize with that benefactor. Designers produce prototypes for feedback, but managers are accustomed to delivering final products, as A. G. Lafley saw before he changed P&G's strategy process. Designers work differently, recruiting their clients onto the design team and helping them see the design for what it is—a prototype. When the AGO's disappointed benefactor grasped that his feedback was integral to the undertaking, he responded with enthusiasm, critiquing each successive iteration, and emerged positively gleeful (like virtually all observers) about the final design, which opened to rapturous reviews in 2008.

But large organizations can't or shouldn't convert themselves entirely to project-oriented, iterative, prototyping design shops. The balanced, design-thinking organization picks the style of work that best fits the task. If the task is to create a company-defining product like the Aeron chair, then fixed, standardized processes will not get the job done.

As a rough rule of thumb, when the challenge is to seize an emerging opportunity, the solution is to perform like a design team: work iteratively, build a prototype, elicit feedback, refine it, rinse, repeat. The team uncovers problems and fixes them in real time, as the process unfolds. On the other hand, running a supply chain, building a forecasting model, and compiling the financials are functions best left to people who work in fixed roles with permanent tasks, people more adept at describing "my responsibilities" than "our responsibilities."

If that sounds like an organization with a baked-in paradox—where one half functions like an accounting firm and the other collaborates like a design shop—well, perhaps it is. But Google shows that a global-scale corporation can balance between the two poles. CEO Eric Schmidt has said that the part of Google that looks like a normal company (sales, marketing, operations) is run like a normal company, but the part that defines what the customer sees and experiences (software coding and engineering) feels more like a design shop, free from top-down control.[8] The challenge for CEOs like Schmidt is to balance freewheeling innovation and buttoned-down operational discipline, validity and reliability, and honing and refining versus jumping to the next stage of the knowledge funnel. While it is not an easy proposition, dealing with this paradox is preferable to being eclipsed by some tiny start-up that stares into the next mystery, while its reliability-fixated rival runs, hones, and refines its existing heuristic or algorithm. The people of Yahoo! know the feeling. It was a lot more fun to own the search space than to watch Google snatch it away.

## Processes That Give Innovation a Chance to Flourish

Two central corporate processes—financial planning and reward systems—are dramatically tilted toward running an existing heuristic or algorithm and must be modified in significant ways to create a balance between reliability and validity. Not unlike the corporate hierarchy, financial planning and reward systems form the hidden infrastructure of the organization, an all-but-invisible force that can promote or stifle design thinking.

*Financial Planning*

Financial planning, budgeting, and budget management are fundamentally reliability-driven processes. They feed on data from the past to predict the future, setting targets for managers to steer toward. They come complete with benchmarks that top management and directors use to assess managerial performance. The best performers run their assigned heuristics or algorithms to meet the outcomes set in the budget. If an operation encounters obstacles to meeting the budget, managers tighten their belts and take extraordinary measures to get back on target. Over the short term, the guiding principle is to produce the consistency of outcomes that boards and stock analysts demand.

The problem is with the long term. For the company to prosper —or even survive—in the long term, it needs a steady stream of insights to push through the knowledge funnel. Only then will it gain the efficiencies that fund the exploration of new mysteries. But the work of converting mysteries to heuristics and heuristics to algorithms is difficult, if not impossible, to financially plan or budget. The past is of little use. The solving of a particular mystery is a unique event that, as our friend Charles Sanders Peirce reminds us, requires a logical leap of the mind. The same holds for the insight that pushes a heuristic to an algorithm. Logical leaps of mind cannot be scheduled; the resources needed to achieve them cannot be determined in advance. Solutions sometimes happen quickly and efficiently, but there is no guarantee.

Companies that truly want to reap the rewards of validity-oriented activities have to take a nontraditional approach to financial planning. Conventional approaches, as we have seen, are tailor-made for those activities involving existing heuristics or algorithms, and the company should plan, budget, and manage them rigorously, aiming for high levels of reliability. For activities aimed at advancing knowledge, however, financial planning should consist only of setting goals and spending limits. Goals define the breakthrough the company is seeking. Spending limits reflect the reality that the company can afford only so much innovation spending in total, and each knowledge advance is worth only so much to the company. The spending limit has to be attuned to the company's entire activity spectrum and the estimated value of the innovation.

In essence, the job of the existing heuristics and algorithms, and those managers running them, is to produce the financial capacity to set the spending limit on innovation high enough for the necessary innovation to be within reach of the organization.

### Reward Systems

The protein that nourishes the ambitious is rewards, both financial and nonfinancial—the latter being primarily the social status earned for a job well done. Typically the highest rewards are conferred on those who run brawny organizations with big-time budgets. The relationship between size and status is pretty straightforward: the larger the revenue and the bigger the staff, the higher one's station and the greater the financial and status payoff. Executives typically measure themselves by the number of people for whom they have direct responsibility and the bottom line that they deliver each year—"I'm important because I run a five thousand-person organization, with annual revenue of $2 billion." And of course, bigger is always better. Status comes from running large, high-revenue business units whose operations have been reduced to reasonably reliable algorithms that produce results on time and on budget. Those are the highest goals, that is, the ones that command the highest compensation. That is why most executives prefer the known to the unknown. It is much easier, safer, and rewarding to run a billion-dollar business than it is to invent one.

Running huge business units is important work. Companies that cannot run, hone, and refine their known heuristics and algorithms on a large scale cannot generate capital to invest in creating the future. But if running those heuristics and algorithms is the only thing that produces monetary rewards and status, companies will not attract people who can invent the future by moving knowledge through the funnel.

Design shops have a much different approach to allocating rewards. Rewards accrue not to those who run big businesses and large staff but to those who solve wicked problems—those with no fixed definition or solution. Check out the workspace of any star designer: desks, credenzas, and shelves are covered with his or her best designs, the ones that solve the most difficult design challenges in the most elegant fashion. The best designers are accorded star status for the challenges they faced, not the revenue they generate. In the business world, Hartmut Esslinger is recognized as the founder and CEO of frog design, an international creative consultancy that counts Hewlett-Packard, Disney, and Nextel among its clients. But in the designers' universe, Esslinger is known and revered as the brains behind the look and feel of the Apple IIc, now in the Whitney Museum of American Art. Says Tim Brown of IDEO, "Success is all about impact. Designers get turned off if their ideas don't make it out into the world."[9]

The organizations that attract talents like Esslinger and Brown give high status to the solving of wicked problems. But there is more to status than rank and title. To keep its people priming the growth engine, P&G imported the designers' ethos of doing meaningful work. The formation of GBS in 1999 was in essence a challenge to the information technology group to become problem solvers. As Filippo Passerini told *Computerworld* magazine, the IT group "is all about identifying what is of business value and determining how technology can help provide that value."[10] Today, his super-geeks are applying virtual-reality technology to improve speed-to-market and improve CRM systems.

By creating a problem-solving culture, Passerini has transformed his organization into a tribe of intrapreneurs who are creating tremendous value for P&G and winning recognition for projects like the integration of Gillette's systems. Marta Foster, the vice president responsible for business-building solutions, said the project, which required a workforce of seven hundred fifty GBS managers, was "incredibly energizing. It's far more meaningful when our work is tightly aligned with the company's strategy. Our people talk about their projects like they're running their own businesses."[11]

Financial planning and reward systems interact in ways that reinforce reliability over validity. Financial planning processes define budgets rigorously and create the basis for rewards. When Jack Welch took over GE, he saw this broken budgeting and rewards system firsthand. As he explained to me in an interview, "If you made your budget, you got a bonus, a pat on the back, and if you missed it, you got a stick in the eye or worse."[12] GE had built a rewards system geared entirely around budget numbers rather than actual success in creating value for company. Reliability was winning the day. The design-thinking organization needs to create flexibility both in its financial planning processes to accommodate exploration activities and in its reward systems to encourage the same. Otherwise, reliability and exploitation will win out.

## Cultural Norms That Reinforce Design Thinking

Design-thinking companies also have to develop new norms—the implicit rules or guidelines that influence behavior. For instance, balancing reliability and validity demands a new way of thinking about constraints. In reliability-driven, analytical-thinking companies, the norm is to see constraints as the enemy: there is never enough capital, customers demand impossibly short intervals, and distributors are always trying to squeeze a little more. It is only natural to complain about the barriers standing in the way of the goal. If reliability is the only goal, then constraints are seen as immovable obstacles to be circumvented. The only thing that matters is to keep running the system that reliably launches products at a fixed level of capital per product, even when long-term value is created by launching the number of products necessary to produce the desired marketplace outcome.

When the goal is validity—that is, arriving at a new desired outcome—constraints take on a different look. "Constraints are opportunities," says Sohrab Vossoughi of Ziba Design. "They force you to be creative. They focus your attention and clarify your thinking."[13] Rather than an enemy, constraints are features that make the task at hand more exciting, the problem more wicked, and the status for releasing the constraint that much loftier. Constraints point the validity-oriented design thinker to the locus of needed innovation. They frame the mystery that needs to be solved. Instead of telling us what we cannot do, constraints help us reframe the problem and discover new opportunities in the process.

Buckminster Fuller is a hero to designers because he was inspired, not discouraged, by a seemingly intractable physical constraint: buildings get proportionally heavier, weaker, and more expensive as they grow larger in scale. The problem inspired him to make a logical leap to a structure that becomes proportionally lighter, stronger, and less expensive as it grows larger in scale—the geodesic dome.

## The Revolt of the Analyticals: Obstacles to Change

Leaders who undertake a thorough overhaul of their organizations' structures, processes, and cultural norms should expect resistance. The vast majority of corporate personnel are trained to be analytical thinkers; for them, design thinking is not even a legitimate category, much less a discipline worth cultivating. Their managers, financiers, and shareholders exert constant pressure to favor reliability over validity. Those stakeholders will, at least initially, withhold rewards from those who champion validity. And they will attempt to discredit validity by demanding proof by inductive or deductive means. That is why any overhaul must begin with design-thinking experiences that reach every corner of the company, as at P&G. There are three major obstacles to creating the productive balance between analytical thinking and intuitive thinking that must be overcome to create a design-thinking organization: preponderance of training in analytical thinking, reliability orientation of key stakeholders, and ease of defending reliability versus validity.

### Preponderance of Training in Analytical Thinking

Only a tiny fraction of managers inhabiting the world of business have any training that would help them be a design thinker. Dan Pink, author of the best-selling *A Whole New Mind: Why Right-Brainers Will Rule the World*, fancifully argued in 2005 that the master of fine arts degree is the new master of business administration. In our world, though, schools don't produce enough MFAs to constitute anything close to a critical mass. American schools graduate only about a thousand MFAs per year versus about a hundred forty thousand MBAs—two orders of magnitude more.[14] If American business is going to be saved by MFAs, we will have to get by with twenty new ones per state per year!

With respect to the one hundred forty thousand MBAs, it is unlikely that even one in a hundred would have been taught anything but inductive and deductive logic during their entire postsecondary education. Many business schools do not merely ignore abductive logic; they inculcate an active hostility to abduction, which is regarded as frivolous. Analytical thinking is presented as not just logically superior but morally superior.

That attitude is carried into the workplace. A client once branded me "willfully negligent" when I argued against putting a question to consumers using a traditional quantitative survey. We would not obtain any useful answers, I maintained, by simply asking, "How would you react to a new service charge?" How would they know how they felt until they saw the charge on their statement? But the client clearly felt that he held the moral high ground by insisting on rigorous research, even if the answers that flowed from that research, reliable as they might be, had no validity.

To executives like my quantitatively minded client, there's something flaky, irresponsible, untidy, and presumptuous about abductive reasoning. Chapter 7 addresses this misconception, which is something most corporations will never do. It will help you develop your own design-thinking capability by viewing your day-to-day work as a seminar in design thinking and in the forces that discourage it.

### Reliability Orientation of Key Stakeholders

Two sets of players critical to corporate operations tend to be heavily oriented toward reliability. By training and inclination, they are slow to reward or even recognize achievements in validity and quick to punish shortfalls in reliability. These stern guardians of reliability are stock market analysts and boards of directors.

Stock market analysts are so enamored of reliability—in their case, defined as hitting their earnings or revenue forecasts—that they actually prefer companies that bring in their earnings on the nose to companies that deliver substantial upside surprises. No matter that the outperformance indicates that the company's strategy is working even better than anyone expected. The upside surprise demonstrates validity, and most analysts can measure only reliability. And in the mind of the analyst, all that matters is what can be measured.

It takes a committed management team to ignore the games played by analysts, a game whose object is to cram an entire universe of information, not all of it coldly quantitative, into the procrustean bed of an earnings model. It takes even more commitment to train the analyst community to understand and appreciate the company's commitment to validity, despite its attendant lesser predictability and consistency. In fact, among U.S. companies, perhaps only Apple Inc. has successfully trained its analysts to value design, largely through the force of Steve Jobs's charisma and the growing popularity of its designs.

Corporate directors might be an even tougher nut to crack than analysts. Boards quite rightly regard themselves as shareholder advocates, and many see the rigorous insistence on reliability as the responsible stewardship of shareholder assets. The leader who seeks to balance reliability with validity should expect resistance from directors and capital markets, whose desire for lasting competitive advantage is often greater than their understanding of how to achieve it.

### Ease of Defending Reliability vs. Validity

In most corporate settings, it is much easier to defend analytical thinking and reliability than it is to defend design thinking and validity. Most executives reached their station in life by studying the past in gruesome detail to chart a course for the future. They have empirical data to support the course they advocate. They are not prepared to evaluate an alternative viewpoint that proceeds not from the basis of what was, but what could be. Such a way of thinking appears fuzzy, dreamy, and more suited to an idealistic undergraduate than a seasoned veteran of the real world. But if a corporation is to bring anything new into the world, it will have to cultivate respect for the sort of logical leap that brought the Aeron into a world that had never seen anything like it.

The challenge for the corporation is to make validity part of the lexicon, overcoming the core training of its employees, boards, and investors. To overcome those challenges, it needs to build in structures and processes that foster, support, and reward a culture of design thinking. "Companies are good at producing 'hothouse tomatoes,'" says John Maeda of the Rhode Island School of Design. "They're perfectly formed and identical, edible but not delicious. Most don't yet know how to integrate the 'heirloom tomato'—the tomato that looks a little different than the rest, lovingly grown by hand with attention to detail, mouth-wateringly delicious. There's a place for both of them at the table." And, he says, a very good reason to go after both. "When people are working on a creative project, they're happy. When a team can come together around a creative cause or a knotty problem, they want to come to work every day. A tough design challenge could be one of the best retention tools a company today has for its best innovators."[15]

## CHAPTER 6

# World-Class Explorers

*Leading the Design-Thinking Organization*

IN THE EARLY 1980S, in a town near Quebec City, a high-school dropout, accordion player, and fire-breather named Guy Laliberté joined a small, itinerant theatrical troupe composed of other jugglers, acrobats, and musicians. By 1984, the group had mounted a successful street festival, and Laliberté began to see the potential for more. Laliberté and his friends were circus performers, but they had no desire to work for a traditional circus. When Laliberté looked at circuses, he saw some remnants of their original allure—the grand spectacle, the potential for joy and surprise. But he also saw the elements that made the circus feel like the dusty remnant of bygone era—the tacky cardboard sets, the smell of sawdust and straw wafting into the audience (among other, less pleasant odors), the sad lives of the circus animals, and lack of a central, cohesive narrative to draw spectators into the experience.[1]

Laliberté began to imagine a new kind of circus, one that captured the magic and spectacle created by the circus performers but replaced the trappings that audiences found dispiriting. Out went the animals, and the many costs and constraints they imposed. Out went the parade of unrelated acts on multiple, garish stages. In came lithe acrobats and contortionists performing a singular-themed show. In, too, came dramatically higher ticket prices, as Laliberté created a show—and price point—that compared favorably with the upscale, grown-up artistry found at the theater, ballet, and opera. He called his new-model circus—part performance art, part comedy routine, part surrealist drama—Cirque du Soleil.

Laliberté had done no research to forecast the size of the market for his new form of circus. How could he? The market did not yet exist. Undeterred, he launched his Cirque du Soleil in 1984 with a thirteen-week, eleven-town tour of Quebec. After some early struggles—including the collapse of the big-top tent before the tour's first show and a chronic shortage of cash—Cirque hit its stride in 1990, with a show called *Nouvelle Expérience*. It was a critical success, and audiences loved it. It was aptly titled; people had never experienced anything like it before. Cirque du Soleil quickly grew from a single show into an organization that simultaneously mounted several different traveling productions. In just a few years, Cirque blossomed from a one-off street festival into an unstoppable international force.

The temptation to keep delivering the same kind of show must have been tremendous. Laliberté and his colleagues had invested almost ten years in developing a show that really worked. But Laliberté somehow resisted the temptation to repeat himself. Throughout Cirque's existence, he has reinvented Cirque's creative and business models time and again, usually over protests that he was fixing what was not broken and that he would destroy the company. He created a permanent show, *Mystère*, in Las Vegas in 1991. As ever, the doubters were out in force. They scoffed at the notion that Vegas gamblers would leave the tables and slot machines long enough to watch two hours of high-concept entertainment and questioned whether Cirque could even pull off a permanent show. "With *Mystère*," Laliberté said in 2006, "we were planting a flower in the desert. It was a big risk and beautiful creative challenge. We had to learn a completely different type of production, but we knew we have the creative ability."[2] Not only did *Mystère* appeal to the Vegas crowd, it became a destination fixture, one of the things visitors to Vegas simply *must* see.

Cirque du Soleil continued to innovate with its formats, with *Delerium* (an arena show that featured reinterpretations of past Cirque performances), with *Zumanity* (a risqué, R-rated show), and with *Love* (a show based entirely on the music of the Beatles that spawned a best-selling CD). All are a departure from Cirque's tested model, yet all have the unique look and feel that defines the Cirque du Soleil brand.

By 2007, Cirque du Soleil was a $600 million-a-year business with four thousand employees and nineteen shows operating either on tour or at a permanent location. Some 70 million people around the world have experienced a Cirque du Soleil show. And for more than twenty-five years, Laliberté has embodied the leader who cultivates design thinking throughout the organization he leads. He stared into a mystery—how can the circus be updated for today's more sophisticated tastes?—and created a new-to-the-world heuristic, the Cirque du Soleil show. Like

RIM's Mike Lazaridis, he played a direct role in guiding the creation of the product, though he became less hands-on as Cirque grew to international scale. Laliberté kept Cirque innovating, doing new things, and pushing the edge.

To do so, he cultivated an environment that consciously put creativity before profit taking. Approximately 70 percent of Cirque's profits are funneled back into R&D and new shows. And he made it his personal responsibility to ensure that reliability did not overpower validity. "A multinational that hires thirty-five hundred persons worldwide, many of them artists who travel constantly, needs a solid organization," explained longtime Cirque executive Jacques Renaud in 2006. "But rules and procedures are a damper on creativity. So, we do have a paradox here. We had to tell the creatives, 'Look, you need strong management; none of you guys is able to run thirteen shows on four continents.' But then, we had to remind legal, finance, or marketing that they wouldn't have much left to manage in the future if the creatives were stifled."[3] Laliberté saw what Cirque could be if it maintained its dynamic balance of strong management and creativity. His leadership nurtured a culture defined by the "ability to start from scratch, from a white page, till we've come up with stuff that nobody had ever dreamed before," said Gilles Ste-Croix, one of Cirque's founding members and a member of Laliberté's inner circle. "And then to risk it, to find ways to make it happen."[4]

Any company dedicated to "starting from scratch, from a white page" needs a design thinker in the CEO's office. The CEO need not be a product design guru, as Lazaridis is at RIM or as Laliberté was for many years at Cirque. Rather, the CEO needs to position himself, as Lazaridis and Laliberté do, as the guardian angel of the balance between reliability and validity in the company, building and protecting the organizational structures, processes, and norms discussed in the last chapter. There are multiple ways to play the role of chief design thinker; the key is to do it. It is a job no one else in the organization can take on.

## Resisting Reliability

Recall that design thinking represents a fruitful balance between intuitive thinking and analytical thinking, between validity and reliability. The need for the CEO to function as the champion of design thinking arises from the tendency of companies to over-weight toward reliability at the expense of validity as they grow.

As companies get bigger and more complex, coordinating their operations becomes more difficult. Senior management becomes more remote from daily operations. Instead of attempting to exercise judgment over a broader and broader domain, senior managers tend to create systems that substitute rules for executive judgment. Those systems—whether they are for budgeting, capital appropriation, product development, or other functions—rely on analytical reasoning. They extrapolate from the past to create plans, targets, and budgets for the future. Using the past as the key reference point is relatively simple and straightforward, allowing senior management to build systems to control an increasing number of regions, product lines, and distribution channels from a distance. The use of systems is seductive, as they both save time and reduce subjectivity. So it is no surprise that external actors, such as boards of directors and stock market analysts, pile on and ask for yet more systems and structures that promote consistency and predictability.

The combined internal and external pressures reinforce the company's reliability orientation.

So, too, do the backgrounds of most CEOs. In a reliability-oriented culture, employees are rewarded based on their ability to deliver on expectations. It makes sense then that the CEO's path to the corner office is often paved with a stellar record of reliability. Traditionally, a disproportionate number of CEOs have risen through the finance function, where ensuring consistency, control, and predictability are the heart of the task. Of course, CEOs who rise through finance can go on to lead design-thinking companies, but to do so, they must recognize their own biases and step outside the structure that helped them become so successful—and to do so even as board members and Wall Street urge them toward ever more reliability.

As their companies grow, CEOs must consciously take on the role of validity's guardian to counter the internal and external pressures toward reliability. They will have no template to follow, as champions of reliability do. The path of the reliability-biased CEO is clear: when faced with a decision about investing in something new and promising, but not in the current budget, just say no. Argue that if something cannot be planned and budgeted in advance, it is not worth doing. Make sure that all jobs have to be formally installed into the permanent structure of the company. And if a project does somehow get the go-ahead, pile it on top of the ongoing activities of someone with a permanent assignment or give it to someone who is unimportant, an underperformer, or on the way out. This way, the organization can read the signals: projects are not important. The CEO can continue to grant the highest status and compensation to those running the biggest businesses, even if they are highly stable algorithms that run like clockwork, and to devalue the tackling of wicked turnaround challenges by giving the managers assigned to them lower status and lower compensation. It is a time-honored formula for enshrining reliability atop the company's hierarchy of values.

The signals the CEO sends establish the company's norms. If the CEO reacts to a problematic constraint by complaining about it, treating it as immutable, and taking suboptimal actions that accept its continued existence, the rest of the company will quickly learn to accept constraints as enemies too powerful to defeat. The CEO who unfailingly demands that executives prove their innovative new ideas with airtight inductive or deductive logic reinforces the norm that these are the only legitimate forms of logic. The CEO who harshly punishes executives who champion innovations that fail, upbraiding them for not doing their homework, ensures that abductive logic will quickly be considered verboten.

The inclination toward reliability is stronger in some parts of the company than others. Typically, the farther the area is from the customer, the greater the reliability bias. Staff functions like finance, information technology, and human resources are farthest away from the customer, while line functions like sales or manufacturing are closer. Left to their own devices, staff functions can and do run roughshod over validity. "We've always done it this way," becomes a magical spell that dead-ends innovation. "We need to have consistency across the entire organization" stops exploration in its tracks. And because the human resources department has a monopoly on its functions, resistance is futile. For internal functions, there is no real market discipline against an overreliance on reliability. The sales function, on the other hand, has beneficial, if sometimes painful, market discipline. A salesperson is the first to know when customers lose their taste for a product or service that has reliably and consistently sold well in the past. Sales will be the first function to argue for a valid proposition, because the reliable one no longer sells.

## Multiple Paths out of the Mystery

If the CEO is not the organization's guardian of the balance between reliability and validity, the long-run sustainability of the company is in question. The role really is that important. But there are lots of productive ways to play the position and play it well. One way to encourage design thinking to take root is to serve as the company's chief designer. The CEO can create a design-friendly culture in large part by taking an active personal role in the design process. This is the Mike Lazaridis model. As the best engineer at RIM, he is ultimately responsible for the portfolio of BlackBerry product designs. His approach to design problems encourages a validity orientation throughout the company. At the other end of the continuum, the CEO can leave the actual design work to others and focus instead on building design-friendly organizational processes into the company, as A. G. Lafley did at P&G. Then there are James Hackett of Steelcase and Bob Ulrich of Target, nondesigners both, who built design-friendly organizational processes and norms into their companies in two distinct but successful ways. In doing so, they made their companies safe havens for design thinking.

## Bringing Design Thinking in from the Outside

James Hackett took over as CEO of Steelcase in 1994 at the ripe old age of thirty-nine. Like Lafley, Hackett had not a minute of design training or background; he was a sales guy, an ex-football-star sales guy in fact. He was also the first nonfamily member to be CEO in Steelcase's proud ninety-six-year history as a family-owned, private company. The largest and most prominent player in the office furniture market worldwide, Steelcase had a rich design heritage. It took root in the 1960s, when, as mentioned in chapter 5, the center of the furniture industry began to shift from western Michigan, home of Grand Rapids–based Steelcase, to the southeastern United States, where labor costs were much lower. To survive, the Michigan-based manufacturers had to focus on design-intensive office furniture. Steelcase, Herman Miller, and Haworth not only survived with this strategy but prospered when the corporate market embraced well-designed furniture at higher prices.

Despite its strong design heritage, Hackett could foresee that as Steelcase grew and went public (which it did in 1998), it could drift away from its tradition of inventing and reinventing the future. The demands for reliability from the board and Wall Street analysts would be hard to ignore or resist. To head off that possibility, he pondered how to instill design thinking into the fabric of his company. His answer came in the form of a longtime partner.

Steelcase had developed a strong working relationship with California-based industrial design firm IDEO. On the basis of its iconic designs, including the first commercial computer mouse and the first laptop computer, IDEO had grown into the country's largest industrial design firm and, based on its lead in industry design awards, quite possibly the world's best. In 1996, Hackett acquired IDEO and made it a wholly owned subsidiary of Steelcase. The purpose of this bold and somewhat controversial move was twofold. First, he wanted to make sure that the design-thinking culture that was so much a part of IDEO would directly influence the culture of the parent Steelcase. And he wanted to signal to his organization that as CEO, he placed a high value on project-based work, abductive reasoning, and a culture of solving wicked problems—the design-thinking attributes of IDEO.

The IDEO acquisition could easily have backfired. There are plenty of examples, across many different industries, of big traditional players acquiring the small innovative entities and then crushing the innovation that made them attractive in the first place. Consider EDS's $600 million purchase of strategy consulting firm A.T. Kearney. EDS acquired Kearney in 1995 hoping that it would infuse the parent company with its creative strategy-making capability. Instead, Kearney's best talent left within a few years, frustrated by the rigid structures, processes, and norms forced on them by their EDS overlords. In 2006, EDS sold Kearney back to management for a nominal price.

Hackett desperately wanted to avoid that outcome. He kept IDEO freestanding, reporting not to the CFO or some line executive but rather to him. IDEO was encouraged to maintain its own structures, processes, and norms, and to teach the Steelcase executives the power of design thinking through joint projects. Rather than wither away postacquisition, as many smaller creative shops tend to do, IDEO blossomed under Steelcase, retained and grew its stellar talent pool, and recently made an agreement to buy back majority control. Hackett acceded to the buyback because the highest priority for him was to foster the things that make IDEO special and to continue to develop the unique benefits those attributes conferred to Steelcase. A CEO who was also his firm's leading advocate for validity, Hackett accomplished the task not by designing but rather by ensuring that the structure, processes, and norms of his firm balanced reliability with validity.

## Creating a Design-Thinking Organization from Within

Then there is Bob Ulrich. In 2008, Ulrich quietly retired after more than twenty years as CEO in what most people would consider one of the dullest and dreariest industries in America: discount retailing. Close your eyes and imagine the typical discount retail store—vast suburban parking lots and characterless cinderblock buildings. Inside, cases of supersized products are stacked to the rafters, amid ramshackle bins of assorted knitwear. Smock-wearing staff members, when spotted, are sullen and unhelpful or painfully cheerful. In the background, droning Muzak is occasionally interrupted with staticky announcements of "special on dishtowels in aisle seven." That was precisely the sort of retailer that Ulrich did *not* want to build. The discount retailer that he envisioned and brought to realization was Target (or "Tar-jhay" if you will) a chain that grew on his watch from 317 stores and $5.3 billion in sales in 1987 to more than 1,600 stores and $63 billion in sales in 2008, when he stepped down as CEO.

Everything about Target is miles away from Walmart, the proto-typical discount retailer. The difference is largely due to Ulrich's leadership and vision.[5]

In a rough and tumble, every-penny-counts industry in which reliability rules, Target—and Ulrich—marched to a different drummer. Ulrich saw to it that Target did not let reliability rule but rather maintained a balance between validity and reliability, constantly innovating where others doubled down on the past. And the big innovation that Ulrich and Target gambled on was embracing design as a competitive advantage.

Target began as a fairly traditional discount retailer, offering department store brands at reduced prices. Part of the Dayton Hudson family of stores, which also once included Marshall Field's, Target faced a critical inflection point in the mid-1980s, just as Ulrich was named president of Target Stores. As Target was growing across the Midwest, Walmart was aggressively expanding into the region and beyond. In those days, Ulrich must have grown increasingly weary of hearing about the singular brilliance of Walmart. Walmart was so much bigger and more valuable than its rivals that discount retailing became known as a stereotypical "winner take all" market, where one firm is so strong that it slowly crushes every rival. In other words, Walmart was considered a category killer.

Walmart chose, then and now, to worship at the altar of reliability. It is all about the algorithm, from the look and feel of the stores, to the mechanics of the distribution system, to the approach of the buyers and merchandisers, to the strategy for expansion. It is not utterly impervious to innovation and change (for instance, its Super-centers now carry groceries), but the basic system is virtually unchanging, and the structure, processes, and norms work against staring into mysteries and developing new heuristics.

As Walmart began to encroach on Target's traditional territory, Ulrich looked at the heuristics associated with retailing—notably the "pile it high and let it fly" merchandising strategy, the plan-o-grams, and other regimented algorithms that Walmart had adopted—and wondered if there was a better way. He stared into the mystery of how Americans want to shop and came to a new answer. Building on the insight that consumers want to feel good about where they shop, even when they shop at a discounter, he created a store designed around the customer experience.

Ulrich wanted Target to become the kind of place in which an affluent shopper might feel good about spending time. The layout of the stores, the branding, advertising, and merchandising all contributed to shaping the experience. Design became the watchword in all of these areas. The stores were reimagined, with clear sight lines, crisp graphics, and clean floors. The branding and marketing adopted a similar clean, crisp aesthetic, coupled with an irreverent tone to create a brand persona very much in keeping with the personae of the customers they sought. But the greatest single insight pertained to the merchandise. Ulrich believed that everyone, no matter their budget, would appreciate and value good design. His plan, then, was not to sell the cheapest goods at the rock-bottom prices, but to deliver well-designed products at a reasonable price point. The Target team went after renowned designers to create affordable versions of their products. Isaac Mizrahi, Philippe Starck, and Todd Oldham came on board, helping forge Target's position as a designer chain, priced for the masses.

The Target slogan, "Expect More, Pay Less," became a strategic filter for senior management's decisions. Building a culture that *Fortune* magazine labeled "highly creative, yet tightly controlled," Target has sought to balance validity and reliability across the business.[6] On the validity front, it has cultivated a creative cabinet—a rotating group of a dozen advisers of varying ages, interests, and nationalities—who are paid a retainer and asked to weigh in on new initiatives from a cereal box design to a new designer relationship. Target has also designed a budgeting mechanism in which year-to-year budgets are not based entirely on past performance. Instead, some portions of the budgets are distributed based on the unproved ideas and projects each department presents for the coming year. The most promising ideas get the most money. That structure has led to dramatic one-off Target experiences, like the temporary floating store installed on New York's Hudson River at Christmas 2002. On the reliability front, it sought to redesign its own infrastructure and back-end processes to be more efficient, so that it could deliver competitive prices on the everyday, national-brand products, like Pepsi and Tide, on which it competed directly with Walmart.

While Walmart focused on a deeply ingrained algorithm, based on logistical excellence and market dominance that it used to strong-arm suppliers into delivering low prices, Target developed a new heuristic. "Walmart's strategy is in many ways more simple than ours," Ulrich said in 2008. "It's more about price and more about mass quantities. It's a hell of a competition, but ours is more dependent on innovation, on design, and on quality."[7]

The new heuristic has served Target well. By 2004, Walmart was beginning to bump up against the limits of reliability, and

Target for the first time experienced higher same-store sales growth and higher sales per square foot than Walmart. Discount retailing was not, after all, a winner-take-all market. Two giants were duking it out, while two giants of an earlier time—Sears and Kmart, which contributed so much to discount retailing's dreary image—withered away. Target stayed in the fight through continuous innovation, even as it grew to the scale necessary to become a worthy and meaningful competitor to Walmart.

No retailer, including Target, is immune to the hazards of standing still in retail. The company now faces a resurgent Walmart, and challenges from newer entrants such as H&M, which have begun to imitate the successful Target heuristic by offering budget-friendly clothing from high-end designers like Stella McCartney and Comme des Garçons. Now that Ulrich has left the company in the hands of new CEO Gregg Steinhafel, his longtime second-in-command, it will be interesting to see if the company seeks to refine its existing heuristics and algorithms or turn its attention to the next mystery. Keeping alive the spirit of innovation and balancing the reliability necessary to compete against Walmart on efficiency with the validity necessary to out-innovate Walmart is Ulrich's legacy as CEO of Target. A merchant, not a designer, he counted on others to design, while he maintained a design-thinking organization.

## The Hybrid Leader

Between the extremes represented by Lazaridis and Laliberté at one end and Lafley, Hackett, and Ulrich at the other, there is a vast expanse of productive middle ground. The specific role played by the CEO is not important. What is important is the protection of validity and the promotion of design thinking. A fine example of successful CEO behavior between the two extremes is Steve Jobs, cofounder and returned CEO of Apple.

Jobs has a long-standing reputation as a visionary designer. He was the cocreator of the Apple II, the forerunner of the Apple Macintosh, and after he left Apple in 1985, the company fell into a succession of disastrous strategies and fratricidal politics. Since his triumphant return as CEO in 1997, Apple has produced a string of design hits including the iMac series, the iPod, and the iPhone. Given his reputation and track record, most people would assume that Jobs functions as Apple's analogue to Laliberté and Lazaridis, chief designer as well as the company's leading advocate of validity. But in actual fact, Jobs operates as more of a hybrid.

While he is credited with launching the iMac line of wildly colored desktop computers upon his return to Apple as CEO, Jobs did not create or even initiate the iMac. Star Apple designer Jonathan Ive conceived and created the iMac, which was essentially ready to go by the time Jobs returned to Apple. Previous management had hemmed and hawed over releasing the over-the-top iMac, which looked like nothing the personal computer industry had ever seen before. PCs were beige or grey boxes whose plain, hard shell masked the complexity inside. But the iMac came in candy colors like turquoise and tangerine, and it showed the guts of the computer through a translucent skin.

When Jobs returned to Apple and saw Ive's bold design, he faced a fundamental choice. From an analytical, reliability-oriented perspective, he would have been able to see that there was no data to suggest that the iMac would have appeal. But the intuitive, validity-oriented argument would have held that people might crave beautiful objects, even when it comes to electronics. If that argument was right, the iMac might actually succeed. Jobs chose decisively for validity and for the iMac, which would become the instrument of Apple's regeneration. But mistakes are inevitable when the CEO prioritizes validity over reliability. Just because something *could* be right does not mean it *must* be. Apple's post-iMac G4 Cube was a rare miss and was discontinued after less than a year on the market. The iPod Hi-Fi sank without a trace.

Missteps aside, the iMac heralded the return of Apple. Soon afterward, Jobs looked at another of Ive's new designs—an MP3 player to be dubbed iPod—and decided that the next Apple product would not be a computer at all, but an entirely different product, which would be a late entrant into a crowded field. All the reliable data said that was a dumb idea. But Jobs chose to believe in what might be, rather than what was; he stared into the mystery of how young people in the twenty-first century wanted to interact with their music and green-lit something that a reliability-oriented system would have strangled in its crib.

Not even Steve Jobs could have predicted how consumers would embrace the iPod. How in the world could one device achieve 70 percent share of such a crowded market? It seemed impossible, but it was achieved thanks to someone (Ive) designing a marvelous product and someone else (Jobs) giving it a chance to succeed. Rather than operating directly as the head designer, Jobs insisted that design thinking would prevail at Apple Computer, which tellingly changed its name in 2007 to Apple Inc. Rather than create the designs himself, he selected great designs created by his organization and approved them for launch. It helps, of course, to have a designer as brilliant as Ive on your team. But would Ive's game-changing creations have ever seen the light of day with someone other than Jobs at the helm?

Jobs was most certainly acting as validity's champion and design thinking's enabler. He played a pivotal role in interpreting consumer perceptions and deciding which products should or should not go forward. In this respect, Jobs is a hybrid. He goes beyond setting up structures, processes, and norms to promote design thinking but no longer engages in design himself. But he is at least as successful as those occupying the extremes of the distribution.

Jobs, Lazaridis, Laliberté, Hackett, and Ulrich demonstrate that different CEOs have different approaches to their role as the organization's chief advocate for the inclusion of validity in decision making. Across each approach, however, is a common theme: a commitment to making the constructive balance of validity and reliability the central component of their job.

Of course, you might argue that a CEO has the kind of leeway to transform his or her organization that the rest of us do not. Setting aside that the CEO might counter with a series of tales of pressure from stockholders, analysts, and board members, let's assume for the moment that is true. How can the rest of us—who don't have the ability to reimagine the structures, processes, and norms of the entire organization—do our best to act as design thinkers on our own jobs, even in a culture that seems designed to stamp out all traces of the balance between validity and reliability? That is the challenge of the next chapter.

# 7

# Getting Personal

*Developing Yourself as a Design Thinker*

IN THE PAST SIX CHAPTERS, I've discussed ways to balance validity and reliability at the organizational level and delved into examples of CEOs who have achieved the balance within their own enterprises. The discussion might lead you to ask whether design thinking is the exclusive domain of the CEO and the members of the senior management team. What can you hope to achieve if you're not a senior manager? What if, for instance, the CEO of your organization carefully protects reliability against validity and steadfastly favors exploitation over exploration? Should you just give up and work at exploiting the current knowledge to produce reliable outcomes? Is that all you can do?

Not by a long shot. It is true that your organization won't advance knowledge as quickly as it could if the CEO made validity a personal protectorate. But that doesn't mean that you can't function as a design thinker, even in the bowels of the most reliability-oriented company. You can work to develop your own design-thinking skills and individually produce more valid outcomes. And you can learn how to work more effectively with non-design thinkers in your organization, rather than engaging in counterproductive battles that result in standoffs, hard feelings, and inaction. Both developing your own designing-thinking skills and learning how to deal more productively with colleagues who are analytical thinkers and intuitive thinkers will help you be a capable and successful design-thinking CEO someday.

## Developing Your Design Thinking Personal Knowledge System

In my previous book, *The Opposable Mind*, I introduced the concept of a *personal knowledge system* as a way of thinking about how we acquire knowledge and expertise.[1] I argued that we all have a personal knowledge system, whether or not we recognize it. For most people, this system develops in an implicit and largely unguided fashion. But that need not be the case. If you work in a reliability-driven, exploitation-oriented organization, your personal knowledge system will naturally develop in a reliability-friendly way, unless you explicitly develop and nurture a balance of reliability and validity. Lack of explicit attention to personal knowledge systems helps ensconce reliability orientation in business organizations and slows movement across knowledge funnels. That is why it is important for you to develop your knowledge system consciously and explicitly.

In *The Opposable Mind*, I explained that your personal knowledge system has three mutually reinforcing components (see figure 7-1). The broadest and most abstract element of that system is

**FIGURE 7-1**

## Your personal knowledge system

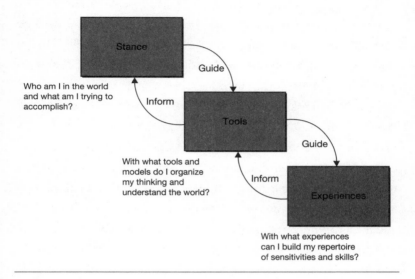

your stance. It is the knowledge domain in which you define how you see the world around you and how you see yourself in that world. For instance, a design thinker sees the world as a place that welcomes new ideas, rather than a hostile environment that punishes change. Remember that designers care profoundly about impact. Their ethos is to do meaningful work. John Maeda of the Rhode Island School of Design captured the optimism of the designer's stance when he told me, "I am encouraged by the potential that artists and designers have to make real changes in the world. Artists and designers have a powerful role in this expansive universe—to take all of the complexity and make sense of it on a human scale."[2] Design thinkers want their ideas to make a difference in the world. Their stance takes for granted that the world can change, and that they, as individuals, can bring about that change. It is a wonderfully open and optimistic way of being.

We all have a stance, and that stance deeply influences our actions. The actions of someone who sees the world as unchangeable and the self as a small cog in a giant machine are very different from the actions of an open and optimistic designer. Yet despite the profound influence our stance has on our actions, we don't often step back to think about what lies beneath that view and behind those actions. Instead, we often take our stance for granted, completely ignoring its impact on our actions and the outcomes they create. We chafe against unsatisfactory outcomes, but rarely go back to explicitly examine how our stance contributed to those outcomes. In fact, because we are so often unconscious of our stance and the assumptions about the world that flow from it, its pushes and pulls are all the more powerful and all the more difficult to resist.

One step down in your personal knowledge system are the tools you use to organize your thinking and to understand your world. There are many tools—from strict analytical frameworks to loose rules of thumb—that can be learned and applied to any number of problems. The tools are efficiency vehicles: without a conceptual tool kit, you would have to tackle every problem from first principles. Theories, processes, and rules of thumb make it possible to recognize and categorize problems, and apply tools to them that have proved effective in similar circumstances in the past. We don't have the need, the time, or the inclination to acquire all the possible tools, so our stance guides which tools we choose to accumulate. Imagine you see yourself as artistically inclined—as someone who loves playing with graphics on a page—and the world as a place in which you can be well paid to pursue your passion. Your stance as a graphics aficionado, for instance, might guide you to enroll in a graphic design program at an art or design school, to gain the formal conceptual tools you'll need to design logos, annual reports, and advertisements.

The final component of the personal knowledge system is experiences. Your experiences form your most practical and tangible knowledge. The experiences you accumulate are the product of your stance and tools, which steer you toward some experiences and away from others. If your stance as a business executive is as a great model builder, and your tools for understanding consumers are sophisticated quantitative models, your experience likely comes from analyzing survey results in your office, not from talking face-to-face with consumers. If instead you see yourself as a people person, skilled at getting consumers to open up about their needs and desires, you will be inclined to build tools for in-home visits and accumulate experiences talking to consumers.

As we accumulate experiences over time, they enable us to hone our sensitivities and skills. *Sensitivity* is the capacity to make distinctions between conditions that are similar but not exactly the same. A chef can make fine distinctions between a piece of meat that is done and one that is not quite. An art critic has the sensitivity to make distinctions between a bold, original talent and a merely competent technician. An experienced equity analyst can read nearly identical financial statements from two different companies, pinpoint where they diverge, and use experience and rules of thumb to accurately predict which will outperform the other.

*Skill* is the capacity to carry out an activity so as to consistently produce the desired result. A skilled chef can consistently cook a steak to the desired state. A skilled art critic can help viewers see the difference between a masterpiece and a lesser work. A skilled stock analyst can consistently distinguish between stocks that will track the overall market and those that will outperform it. True skill, it is important to note, does not merely produce the reliable result; it reliably produces the desired result.

Skills and sensitivities tend to grow and deepen in concert. As you repeat a task, you are inclined to build what you learned from the repetition into the next iteration until you develop a consistent technique. An improved technique sharpens your skill, making you faster and more accurate. And as you repeat a task, you learn to make finer and finer distinctions between levels of quality, so that an experienced chef can tell almost by instinct when a steak is blue and when it's rare.

People at all levels of an organization have the opportunity to develop their skills and sensitivities thoughtfully and directly through their experiences. A. G. Lafley developed advanced skills and sensitivities over a quarter-century at Procter & Gamble before he took over the top job. He began as a brand assistant, fresh from Harvard Business School after a five-year stint in the U.S. Navy. He had already developed a stance that said the world would welcome new ideas, and that he was capable of generating those ideas. He acquired a set of tools over his career—supply-chain management in the navy, general management theory from Harvard Business School, and brand-building techniques from the masters at P&G— which he employed to good effect. Finally, he gained experiences that developed both his skills and his sensitivities. He experienced running large and highly profitable product lines that needed to innovate and grow; he experienced introducing a relatively unknown brand against a dominant traditional player; and he experienced firsthand how the decisions made by marketing managers affect the sales and distribution teams. He experienced running brands with profoundly different profit dynamics—learning that you can't charge more than $2 for a four-roll package of Charmin toilet paper, but you can charge more than $30 for a small vial of Olay Regenerist when it is branded in just the right way. The multitude of experiences developed Lafley's skills and sensitivities as he moved up the P&G hierarchy; what's more, they reinforced his stance and influenced his continuing development of new and better tools.

Personal knowledge develops as a system because its three elements influence one another. Stance guides tool acquisition, which in turn guides the accumulation of experience. The flow, however, is not one-way. Experiences inform the acquisition of more tools. As experience leads us to acquire new tools, we add depth and clarity to our stance. When a person starts in a given direction, that direction is likely to be reinforced and amplified, not diminished or altered. This can happen for good or bad; that is, the spiral can be beneficial or detrimental. A narrow and defensive stance will lead to acquisition of extremely limited tools and extremely limiting experiences. Those experiences then feed back into the acquisition of even more limited tools and the formation of an even narrower stance. A more expansive stance will lead to the acquisition of more powerful tools and challenging learning experiences, which will promote more tool acquisition and a more powerful stance.

Neither a downward nor upward spiral is foreordained. Your personal knowledge system—your stance, tools, and experiences—is under your control. You have wide latitude as to how to develop your personal knowledge system. You might not be able to change your height or DNA, but as long as you can change your stance, you can change the tools and experiences you use to develop your design-thinking capacity.

## The Design Thinker's Personal Knowledge System

The design thinker's personal knowledge system is distinctive along all three dimensions: stance, tools, and experiences. It generates a self-reinforcing spiral that values validity and exploration; it develops the stance, tools, and experiences that make a design thinker capable of designing new ways of doing business and new businesses. Rather than perpetuating the past, the design thinker creates the future. "Which project is my favorite?" asks the brilliant Sohrab Vossoughi, founder of Ziba Design. "The answer is always the same—the next one."[3]

### Stance

Design thinkers are under no delusion that the world adores validity and encourages exploration. They fully understand that the world they live in substantially favors reliability over validity, consistency over innovation. They also recognize that honing and refining knowledge within the confines of its current stage in the knowledge funnel is what the world most readily permits and consistently rewards—and that exploitation is essential to a well-performing enterprise.

Despite that view of the world, design thinkers seek to balance validity and reliability. They don't ignore reliability by any stretch, but they will trade off against reliability in order to reach a valid answer. In addition, the design thinker lives to advance knowledge to the next stage in the funnel. Advancing knowledge is a core drive, a source of pride and happiness. Although validity is trickier and more uncertain than reliability, the design thinker understands that one without the other does not make a sustainably advantaged enterprise.

Again, speaking to designers can help illustrate the core of the design thinker's stance. IDEO's Tim Brown explains the difference between the reliability mind-set and the validity mind-set, as he sees it: "Most managers are trying to design variance out of the system, and cannot handle a process which starts off not knowing where it will eventually get. Poor design briefs are not normally the ones with too many constraints (although that can be an issue), but the ones that take all opportunity for discovery and surprise away."[4] The design thinker has a stance that seeks the unknown, embraces the possibility of surprise, and is comfortable with wading into complexity not knowing what is on the other side.

The design thinker's stance, however, does not demand validity at any cost. The best designers recognize the importance of reliability in steering them away from flakiness. "Good designers are as anal about the things that matter to them as the most anal bookkeeper in your accounting department," says Microsoft's Bill Buxton. "When in a time-crunch, often the first thing that the professional designer will do is block off a schedule—precisely so that they know how much time they have to play and explore before they have to deliver. Design is not art; it is about pragmatic compromise rather than perfection. Behind the apparent chaos is discipline. It just appears as chaos because the calculus is different than that of other disciplines."[5] Again, taking the stance of the design thinker leads us to strike a balance between validity and reliability by explicitly seeking out validity, not by eliminating reliability altogether.

For the manager, the first step to acquiring a design thinker's stance is to be conscious of your own stance. Think about the decisions you make and explicitly ask yourself about the assumptions and beliefs behind them. Then compare your stance to the design thinker's embrace of complexity and willingness to be surprised. Do you see an opportunity to move closer to the design thinker's stance? The first move in that direction may be as simple as reminding yourself, again and again until it becomes second nature: "My job is to balance reliability with validity."

*Tools*

The key tools of design thinkers are observation, imagination, and configuration. This troika of tools follows consistently from the design-thinking stance.

The first of the three is *observation*—deep, careful, open-minded observation. Since design thinkers are looking for new insights that will enable them to push knowledge forward, they must be able to see things that others don't (for example, patterns that can help turn a mystery into a heuristic). This requires careful watching and listening in a way that is responsive to the subject, as an ethnographer would. An ethnographer attempting to understand how youngsters in China think about their handheld phones would watch them use their phones before even asking a single question. And when appropriate to ask, the question would likely be of the form: "I saw you punch one button repeatedly; you looked frustrated. Then you flipped the phone closed and opened it again. Why were you doing that? What were you thinking? How did it make you feel?"

That's a very different approach from asking, "What are the top five things that matter to you about your handheld phone?" Now, any phone manufacturer would love to know which five things matter most to young users. But to ask for a ranked list from phone users would be to ask them to do the designers' jobs for them. Users can and do conceptualize their feelings about their handhelds, but rarely in the form of a top-five list. That list is for the designer to compile—and only after diving deep into the user experience.

Deep, user-centered understanding, using the techniques of the ethnographer, is an essential tool of the design thinker. Shallow understanding that is oriented to confirming and perpetuating the current model causes knowledge to ossify rather than move forward. As a manager, if you want to understand your customers, think carefully about the kind of data you want and how best to get it. Embrace the idea of spending time with your customers. Imagine you work at one of the big three automakers. How could you better understand what American consumers really want in their cars? You could look at the list of best-selling cars and try to infer what it is about the Honda Civic that is so appealing. Or you could ask a focus group of customers how important things like gas mileage and color selection are to them. Chances are that you would end up exactly where the Big Three are today. Consider, instead, actually spending time with your customers and those of your competitors, going to their houses and garages to listen to them talk about their cars, how they make them feel, what makes them happy, and what frustrates them. From these visits, you would be able to distill deeper insights into the mystery of your changing customers than analytical thinking could ever get you.

The second tool of the design thinker is *imagination*. At first blush, it may seem that imagination is simply a natural act of the human mind, rather than a tool. It's true that we all have imagination. Yet for many of us, it is underdeveloped. Design thinkers programmatically hone imagination into a powerful tool, one comprised of an inference and testing loop.

To move from one stage on the knowledge funnel to the next, one has to experience, through observation, data that is neither consistent with nor explained by the current models—as Dr. Scherer has done in analyzing the genes of people with ASD (see chapter 2). When faced with that data, one must make an inference to an explanation. It is a guess that constitutes the best explanation one can devise given the data, which is insufficient to yield a statistically significant finding. That inference-making process is what we call abductive reasoning, Charles Sanders Peirce's third form of logic.

It is a powerful form of reasoning about the world that, as we have seen, is underutilized and underdeveloped in the business domain in favor of deductive and inductive logic. Businesses don't reject abductive reasoning merely because they're hidebound; after all, abduction does have a weakness we've already explored, which is that ideas based on abductive reasoning can't be proved in advance. There is a decent chance they could be just plain wrong. This is why the inference-testing loop is so important. Here, the design thinker tests the breakthrough inference by producing a prototype and observing whether it operates as desired or expected. Typically, even with a talented abductive thinker, the initial prototype falls well short of what's desired.

Those shortcomings, viewed from the design thinker's stance, offer the opportunity to infer what would make the prototype better, giving rise to a succession of new tests, new inferences, new prototypes, until we arrive at a winning design—whether that is a design of a product, service, customer experience, or organization. In your role, you can choose to make prototyping and testing part of your lexicon. Just as you explicitly embrace abductive thinking, asking yourself what could be true, you can commit to testing and retesting that inference.

The final tool of the design thinker is *configuration*—translating the idea into an activity system that will produce the desired business outcome. This is essentially the design of a business that will bring the abductively created insight to fruition. Without that, all the observation and imagination will have no meaningful payoff. The master of configuration is Steve Jobs, who created an activity system for the iPod, including iTunes and Apple stores. The system made iPod a compelling product, exceedingly hard to replicate and highly profitable. (See figure 7-2.)

For a manager, the configuration step is to ask how your insight and new solution fit into the larger scheme of the business in which you operate. The activity system you create may relate only to your department or project. But even within that limited sphere, you can build a model to test and verify.

FIGURE 7-2

## Apple's iPod activity system

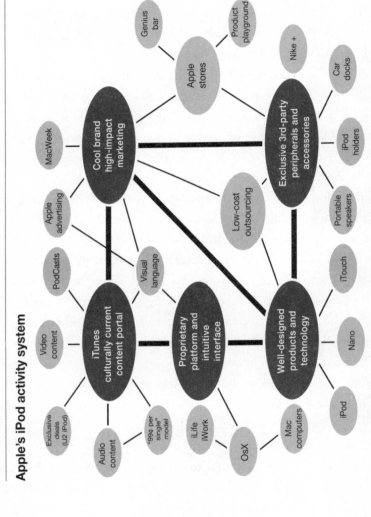

## *Experiences*

To be a better design thinker, consciously use your experiences to deepen your mastery and nurture your originality. That advice probably sounds familiar to readers of *The Opposable Mind*. Integrative thinking—the subject of that book—and design thinking have much in common. Integrative thinking is the metaskill of being able to face two (or more) opposing ideas or models and instead of choosing one versus the other, to generate a creative resolution of the tension in the form of a better model, which contains elements of each model but is superior to each (or all). Design thinking is the application of integrative thinking to the task of resolving the conflict between reliability and validity, between exploitation and exploration, and between analytical thinking and intuitive thinking. Both ways of thinking require a balance of mastery and originality.

Mastery, whose markers are organization, planning, focus, and repetition, requires repeated experiences in a particular domain. Because masters in their domain have seen particular phenomena before and know what they mean, they don't have to interpret every sensation or input from scratch as a novice would. In the infinite morass of data, they can pull out the few salient points that make a difference and mentally map their causal relationships. When a customer complains to an automobile mechanic that the car accelerates sluggishly when the light changes and shudders when decelerating, the mechanic, drawing on personal experience, will know the first part to check for a problem is the fuel line. Because the mechanic has encountered this problem many times before, the mechanic knows from experience how to structure the investigation to resolve the problem quickly and without wasted effort.

Some contexts don't reward the repetition, structuring, and planning that are the hallmarks of mastery. Those nonstandard contexts require the creation of a new approach or solution; they require originality. Originality demands a willingness to experiment, spontaneity in response to a novel situation, flexibility to change directions as information dictates, and responsiveness to opportunities as they present themselves, even if they're unexpected. Rooted as it is in experimentation, originality openly courts failure. It's important to become comfortable with the processes of trial and error and iterative prototyping, or you'll be tempted to focus on the less risky mode of mastery, to the exclusion of originality.

Mastery without originality becomes rote. The master who never tries to think in novel ways keeps seeing the same thing the same way. In this manner, mastery without originality becomes a cul-de-sac. By the same token, originality without mastery is flaky, if not entirely random. The power is in the combination.

Successful design thinkers—at any level of the organization—will devote time and practice to mastering the specific tools and skills associated with their role. They will strive to understand how things work within their system. But, at the same time, they will consciously and explicitly seek out opportunities to try new things and test their boundaries. Just as reliability pushes out validity, an overemphasis on mastery can obliterate considerations of originality. Make a continuing, conscious effort to counteract this tendency by nurturing your originality, even in the smallest of ways. Flex your creative muscles, volunteer for a committee

**FIGURE 7-3**

### Design thinker's personal knowledge system

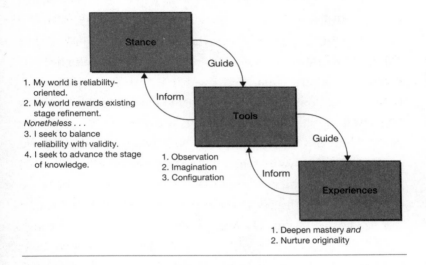

outside your area of expertise, and stretch outside of your area of mastery.

Overall, the knowledge system of a design thinker—someone who sets out to design business rather than to replicate what currently exists—has specific, unique components of stance, tools and experiences (see figure 7-3).

## Working More Effectively with Different Colleagues

Since the business world is a reliability-oriented place, in the bulk of organizations most of your colleagues will be reliability-driven analytical thinkers. But the organization also needs validity-driven people to keep the organization from stagnating through overexploitation and underexploration. The problem is that validity-driven people make the reliability-driven folks profoundly nervous. And the reliability-driven folks depress the heck out of the validity-driven folks.

That means that if you want to be a designer of business and an effective rather than frustrated design thinker, you need to become skilled at working productively with reliability-driven analytical thinkers who dominate the hierarchy and the validity-driven intuitive thinkers who are often brought in to "get the organization out of the box." Otherwise, nothing will get done except that you and those on the two extremes will annoy each other.

There are five things that the design thinker needs to do to be more effective with colleagues at the extremes of the reliability and validity spectrum: (1) reframe extreme views as a creative challenge; (2) empathize with your colleagues on the extremes; (3) learn to speak the languages of both reliability and validity; (4) put unfamiliar concepts in familiar terms; and (5) when it comes to proof, use size to your advantage. For each of these five pieces of advice, there are specific thoughts on applying the lesson to reliability-driven and validity-driven colleagues.

## 1. Reframe Extreme Views as a Creative Challenge

Design thinkers generally love nothing more than a tricky and complicated design challenge. They welcome constraints, which help them define the challenge and push their ideas in unexpected directions. They enjoy the opportunity to advance knowledge to the next stage of the knowledge funnel. However, faced with colleagues at the extremes of reliability or validity, design thinkers often take an unproductive approach. They are inclined to dismiss their analytical colleagues as squares and philistines who can't appreciate what needs to be done and their intuitive colleagues as flighty and impractical folks who threaten organizational order.

Rather than viewing these colleagues as problems and attempting to wish them away, the design thinker needs to embrace the challenges of the extremes as a wonderful design challenge that is as exciting as any other managerial design challenge. For reliability-focused colleagues, the design thinker has to embrace the challenge of finding creative ways to help them see the value of accepting some validity into the path forward. And for validity-focused colleagues, the design thinker has to embrace the challenge of finding creative ways to bring managerial order to their work without destroying its integrity.

Dealing productively with colleagues on both extremes is not a problem to be rued but rather a design-thinking task of central importance, one which requires the design thinker's best work.

### 2. Empathize with Your Colleagues on the Extremes

The only way to design a compelling solution is to really understand the user. It's almost impossible to design something compelling for someone you don't respect or wish to understand. Architects' offices are cluttered with filing cabinets full of unrealized, unbuilt houses, all designed for clients whom the architects saw as philistines. The designs, whatever their merits, are an indictment not of the client but of the architect, whose lack of respect for the user prompted the rejection. The architect finds consolation in the brilliance of the design, explaining away its stillborn fate by arguing that the client was unworthy of it, forgetting whose job it was to understand the client's needs and wishes and, under those constraints, design a beautiful home.

In contrast, the effective design thinker empathizes with colleagues who exist at the extremes of analysis and intuition, seeking to achieve deep understanding of their positions and uncover the greatest range of options for a compelling solution. What are the colleague's greatest hopes? What keeps him or her up at night worrying? What are the minimum acceptable conditions for the colleague to embrace a design solution? How much risk is the colleague willing to absorb? The design thinker can answer these questions with either empathy or disdain.

What keeps the reliability-driven colleague up at night? The ineffective design thinker sees the colleague's desire as proverbial ass covering. The effective designer thinker sees the colleague's desire to protect employees from the consequences of a reckless decision. In the case of the schism between the worldview of the design thinker and the analytical thinking colleague, a better, more empathetic understanding enables the design thinker to probe what distinguishes a reckless decision from a sensibly aggressive decision, seeking to understand the distinction from the reliability-driven colleague's standpoint. Only with such empathy can the design thinker forge a solution that productively meets the reliability-driven colleague's needs.

Likewise, the only way the design thinker can create a productive organizational context for intuitive thinkers is to empathize with them. Those seeking validity are not trying to be dangerous and worrisome; they are attempting to make sense of fuzzy data, qualitative insights, and judgment. Intuitive thinkers see things that escape analytical thinkers. Only by empathizing with validity-seeking thinkers—and really understanding the way in which they think—can the design thinker be capable of devising managerial structures that address the organizational need for both reliability and validity.

### 3. Learn to Speak the Languages of Both Reliability and Validity

To empathize, one needs to communicate. But analytical thinkers and intuitive thinkers speak different languages. Analytical thinkers speak the language of reliability, because they put a high priority on the production of consistent, predictable outcomes. They frequently use words such as proof, regression analysis, certainty, best practices, and deployment. Intuitive thinkers speak the language of validity, because they put a high priority on the production of outcomes that delight, whether or not they are consistent and predictable. They frequently use words such as breakthrough, new to the world, and, yes, awesome. But to analytical thinkers, these words connote danger, uncertainty, and guesswork—things that encourage, if not compel, them to say no. In such circumstances, it is incumbent on the design thinker to learn the languages of both extremes. Otherwise, design thinkers might as well be speaking Greek to an Italian audience.

Like anyone else who takes a job in another country and needs to learn the local language in order to function, design thinkers need to learn the language of reliability to be successful in communicating with reliability-driven colleagues and the language of validity to communicate with validity-driven colleagues. If the design thinker comes from a business training and background, the need will likely be to learn the language of validity. If the design thinker comes from design training, the need will likely be to learn the language of reliability. And what is the best way to learn another language? It is to spend time with those who speak the language you wish to acquire, in their environment. Just listen, as if it is truly important and with empathy, and you will learn the language in no time.

### 4. Put Unfamiliar Concepts in Familiar Terms

When a reliability-driven colleague cares primarily about substantiation based on past events and a validity-driven colleague cares only about substantiation based on future events, both face a challenge in communicating ideas compellingly. What tools can the design thinker use to bridge the gap? To help the reliability-driven colleague, the best tool for the design thinker to encourage is analogy: for the design thinker to craft a story that takes an existing idea in operation elsewhere and show the analytical thinker how it resembles the novel idea being proposed—not exactly the same, but similar enough. That helps the reliability-driven analytical thinker see the idea as less threatening and problematic.

I learned the hard way as a strategy consultant that if I didn't use analogy to help a reliability-driven client I would fail to be convincing. My lesson occurred some years ago, when the Canadian banking industry was undergoing radical change. New regulations allowed the big retail banks to buy up the independent brokerage firms. The result was a boon for the consulting industry, as the big banks tried to integrate the structure and culture of their new brokerage arms. One such bank asked me to develop a strategy for its high-net-worth customers. Previously, the bank had been limited to providing these customers with checking accounts, guaranteed investment certificates, mortgages, and traditional retail banking products. Now that it could offer brokerage services to these same customers, the bank wanted an integrated strategy for serving this lucrative segment.

When they thought about the bank's high-net-worth customers, the bank executives visualized customers who looked a lot like themselves: corporate execs, lawyers, and partners at the biggest professional service firms. The initial strategy of the bank focused on these customers and served them in its biggest downtown branches with special, splendidly appointed "private banking" offices.

As my team and I dug into the data, it became clear to us that this group, though undeniably affluent, were not a desirable set of customers. They selected a limited and quite vanilla-flavored suite of services, and they were picky, demanding, and price sensitive. But there was another group of high-net-worth individuals who were underserved and seemed willing to pay for a broader array of services. They were entrepreneurs and partners from small legal and accounting firms, often living and working in the suburbs that ringed Canada's larger cities. These folks had a much more complex set of needs and refused to observe any dividing line between their personal and business finances. They wanted mortgages for their homes and for their investment properties, they wanted to co-invest with clients and partners, and they didn't want to have to bounce from one narrow specialist in the bank to another to get a deal done. They also did not want to have to drive into the city to a fancy main branch filled with high-backed chairs and wood-paneled walls, all bought with *their* service fees. Instead, they wanted highly integrated, personal service in their own neighborhood, with no divide between their commercial and personal banking services. None of the Canadian banks had a compelling service package to offer this potentially valuable market. I crafted a strategy that focused on serving this dynamic segment.

At the final presentation, I proudly presented our radical new strategy. At the end, the CEO nodded solemnly and asked, "Have any of the other banks done this?" I answered brightly, "No, you would be the very first." I was certain that this news would seal the deal. It didn't. The meeting was over. The risk-averse CEO could not imagine gambling on an unproven and utterly unreliable idea.

My mistake was to speak to the CEO in the language of validity, which practically invited him to reject my argument out of hand. Had I had more empathy with my client and understood the language of reliability, I might have responded to his query using an illustrative example. I might have said, "None of our domestic competitors have done this. But a variant of this approach has been used by some of the best-performing European private banks for some time. It isn't exactly the same, but it bears important similarities. And recall, our bank has succeeded in the past when it has taken an idea from outside our home market and introduced it here." Bridging the language gap will not eliminate the apparent risk of an idea, but it presents the unfamiliar in a familiar, reliability-oriented framework. An analogy or story helps reliability-driven colleagues see that you are not substantiating your argument based exclusively on future events but in part on past events.

To help the validity-driven colleague, the best tool for the design thinker is to encourage the sharing of data and reasoning, but not conclusions. Reliability-oriented thinkers are inclined to crunch all the data that they see as relevant, come to a firm conclusion on the analysis, and then impose that conclusion on everyone else. Intuitive thinkers, though, are likely to object that their analytical-thinking colleagues have considered only a small fraction of the relevant data; they are overlooking or consciously ignoring plenty of relevant data that is hard to measure and quantify. If analytical thinkers attempt to impose their conclusions on their validity-driven colleagues, they will cause them to feel that it is impossible to develop a truly innovative solution because so many important design features are being ignored.

However, if the reliability-driven colleagues don't at least share their data and reasoning with their intuitive-thinking counterparts, the two cannot hope to understand each other. That gap will make it much less likely that the design thinker will be able to forge a design solution that both the analytical and intuitive thinkers will find acceptable. For analytical thinkers, sharing their data and reasoning, but stopping short of imposing conclusions, helps the design thinkers come up with a solution to which all parties can say yes. While the end design may make their reliability-driven colleagues nervous on the margin, it will be less likely to be a design that they feel compelled to reject out of hand as too scary and dangerous.

### 5. When It Comes to Proof, Use Size to Your Advantage

Even with careful use of language and employment of analogies, proof is the biggest problem. Validity seekers don't traffic in proof of the sort that reliability-seeking colleagues want, which is substantiation based on past events. Validity seekers simply can't prove in advance that their ideas will work.

There is good news and bad news about the future. The bad news is that a year from now is the future and, from a proof standpoint, what happens then is irrelevant. The good news is that a year from now, that year is the past. This nuance is critical to reliability-driven colleagues. Design thinkers can convince their colleagues to bite off a piece of what they would like to do and say, "Here is my prediction of what will happen. Let's watch next year to see whether it does or not." If they agree to bite off that chunk and the design thinkers' predicted results happen over the year, the reliability-driven colleague will gain confidence in them and their ideas. What was in the future a year ago is in the past today. The key for design thinkers is to turn the future into the past, because the reliability-driven colleague sees the future as the enemy and the past as a friend.

Validity seekers resist biting off a little piece because it feels to them that any parsing or phasing of the solution will destroy its integrity. Most would rather have everything done in one swoop and not look back. But because that sort of uncertainty is anathema to analytical thinkers, design thinkers, if only out of self-interest, need to develop skills in biting off as little a piece as possible. That affords them the best chance to turn the future into the past.

When dealing with intuitive thinkers, on the other hand, design thinkers need to stretch to bite off a piece that is big enough to give innovation a chance. They have to listen to an argument from their validity-seeking colleagues that they will have to realize some significant portion of the whole to know whether the design will in fact work.

From the middle, the design thinkers need to develop their skills in helping both reliability- and validity-driven colleagues to design right-sized experiments that productively turn the future into the past.

## Getting Along

In many respects, the advice for getting along is quite generic: appreciate the legitimate differences; empathize; seek to communicate on their terms, not yours, using tools with which they would be familiar; and stretch out of your comfort zone toward those of others. Getting along has never been and will never be rocket science. But the world is full of conflicts, including the uneasy relationship between intuitive thinkers and analytical thinkers, between the forces of validity and reliability. The relationship should be highly productive, and the design thinker can help make it so.

Developing your design-thinking capabilities is a continuous exercise in balance. The exploration of valid solutions will find its counterweight in the ability to exploit those solutions efficiently. The inner-directed work of developing your stance, tools, and experiences as a design thinker will be integrated with the outer-directed work of communicating and collaborating with colleagues who tilt strongly toward reliability (or, less often, validity). The exciting pursuit of solutions to wicked problems will alternate with the sober calculation of the business value of solving the problem. As you grow more sure-footed and adept at maintaining the design thinker's balance, you will gain fluency in both the allusive poetry of intuitive discovery and the precise prose of analytical rigor. And as you learn the many ways in which design thinking creates value for a business, you will also discover that design thinking creates meaning for your life.

# Notes

## Chapter 1

1. Information on McDonald's was drawn from a number of sources, notably Michael Arndt, "The Creator of McWorld," *Business Week*, July 5, 2004, 18; Lewis Lord, "The McHistory of America," *U.S. News & World Report*, December 27, 1999, 53; http://www.time.com/time/time100/builder/profile/kroc.html; http://www.aboutmcdonalds.com/mcd/our_company/mcd_history.html

2. Bono made this remark while accepting Record of the Year at the 43rd Annual Grammy Awards, February 21, 2001.

3. http://www.metacritic.com/music/artists/u2/allthatyoucantleave behind.

4. See James March. "Exploration and Exploitation in Organizational Learning," *Organization Science* (February 1991): 71–87.

5. In 2007, Steelcase agreed to sell controlling interest in IDEO to IDEO's management team, transitioning ownership over a five-year period.

6. Saul Bellow, *The Actual* (New York: Viking, 1997).

## Chapter 2

1. For more on Dr. Stephen Scherer, see http://www.tcag.ca/scherer/.

2. All of the quotes from Dr. Stephen Scherer in this chapter come from a discussion with the author, November 6, 2008.

3. For more on the Human Genome Project, see http://www.ornl.gov/sci/techresources/Human_Genome/home.shtml and https://www.celera.com/celera/history.

4. Ian Davis and Elizabeth Stephenson, "Ten Trends to Watch in 2006," *The McKinsey Quarterly* (January 2006).

5. Historical stock prices retrieved from http://finance.yahoo.com/. Other details from: David Friend, "Research In Motion Shares Drop 26 Per cent after Missing Analyst Expectations," *The Canadian Press*, September 26, 2008, and Matt Hartley, "RIM Has Its Bell Rung," *Globe and Mail*, September 26, 2008.

6. Daniel A. Levinthal and James G. March, "The Myopia of Learning," *Strategic Management Journal* (Winter 1993): 105.

7. "We shape our buildings, and afterwards our buildings shape us;" Winston Churchill, British House of Commons, October 28, 1943.

*Chapter 3*

1. Unless otherwise indicated, all quotes from Mike Lazaridis in this chapter come from a discussion with the author, April 2, 2009.

2. "Research In Motion Reports Fourth Quarter and Year-End Results for Fiscal 2009," Research In Motion press release, April 2, 2009.

3. Tim Brown, "Design Thinking," *Harvard Business Review*, June 2008, 86.

4. Bertrand Russell, *Wisdom of the West* (London: Macdonald, 1959).

5. Cheryl Misek, *The American Pragmatists* (London: Oxford University Press, forthcoming).

6. Michael Dell, in conversation with the author as part of the Rotman School of Management's Integrative Thinking Experts Speaker Series, September 21, 2004.

7. Brian Banks and Mark Evans, "Two Men and Their Baby," *Financial Post Business*, November 2006, 32–38.

*Chapter 4*

1. Historical stock prices retrieved from http://finance.yahoo.com/.

2. Marian Stinson, "Procter and Gamble Awash in a Sea of Selling," *Globe and Mail*, March 29, 2000, B18.

3. Daniel Eisenberg, "Trouble in Brand City," *Time*, March 20, 2000, 47.

4. Patrick Larkin and Ken Stammen, "Investors agonize over P&G stock slip; Analysts: Recovery could take 3 years," *Cincinnati Post*, March 17, 2000, 5C.

5. Per the *Financial Times* Global 500 rankings.

6. All of the quotes from Claudia Kotchka in this chapter come from a discussion with the author and Jennifer Riel, November 20, 2008.

7. See Bill Buxton, *Sketching User Experiences: Getting the Design Right and the Right Design* (San Francisco: Morgan Kaufman, 2007), 63.

8. C. West Churchman, "Wicked Problems," *Management Science*, vol.14, no. 4 (December 1967).

9. Bill Buxton, correspondence with the author, October 17, 2008.


*Chapter 5*

1. http://www.hermanmiller.com/CDA/SSA/Product/1,1592,a11–c1639-p60,00.html.

2. Joseph Hooper, "The Air Chair," *Esquire*, April 1997, 106.

3. Malcolm Gladwell, *Blink: The Power of Thinking Without Thinking* (New York: Little, Brown and Company, 2005).

4. http://www.hermanmiller.com/CDA/SSA/Product/1,1592,a10–c440-p8,00.html.

5. All of the quotes in "The De Prees of Herman Miller" box are from a Hugh De Prees speech given at the Rochester Institute of Technology (Rochester, NY), 1965.

6. As related to the author in conversation, 1993.

7. David Kelley, correspondence with the author, October 30, 2008.

8. Roger Martin, "Tough Love: Business Wants to Love Design, But It's an Awkward Romance," *Fast Company*, October 2006.

9. Tim Brown, correspondence with the author, October 9, 2008.

10. Julia King, "Getting the Message Out," *Computerworld*, February 19, 2007.

11. As quoted in Roger Martin, "Tough Love: Business Wants to Love Design, But It's an Awkward Romance."

12. Jack Welch, in conversation with the author as part of the Rotman School of Management's Integrative Thinking Experts Speaker Series, September 12, 2005.

13. Sohrab Vossoughi, correspondence with the author, October 20, 2008.

14. U.S. Department of Education, National Center for Education Statistics, 2003–04 Integrated Postsecondary Education Data System (IPEDS), Fall 2004.

15. John Maeda, correspondence with the author, October 31, 2008.


*Chapter 6*

1. Information on Guy Laliberté and Cirque du Soleil was drawn from a number of sources, notably: Benoit Aubin, "Disney of the New Age," *Maclean's*, June 2006, 22; David Dias, "Entrepreneur of the Year," *Financial Post Business*, December 2006, 56; Konrad Yakabuski, "The Greatest Canadian Company

on Earth," *Report on Business Magazine,* August 2007, 56; Linda Tischler, "Join the Circus," *Fast Company,* July 2005, 52.

2. As quoted in Dias, "Entrepreneur of the Year."

3. As quoted in Aubin, "Disney of the New Age."

4. Ibid.

5. Information on Bob Ulrich and Target was drawn from a number of sources, notably: "Business: On Target," *The Economist,* May 5, 2001, 1; Mike Duff, "End of an Era, Beginning of a Legacy," *Retailing Today,* April 14, 2008, 16; Jennifer Reingold, "Target's Inner Circle," *Fortune,* March 31, 2008, 74; Julie Schlosser, "How Target Does It," *Fortune,* October 18, 2004, 100; http://sites.target.com/site/en/company/page.jsp?contentId=WCMP04-032391.

6. Reingold, "Target's Inner Circle."

7. Ibid.

*Chapter 7*

1. Roger Martin, *The Opposable Mind* (Boston: Harvard Business School Press, 2007), 91–106.

2. John Maeda, correspondence with the author, October 31, 2008.

3. Sohrab Vossoughi, correspondence with the author, October 20, 2008.

4. Tim Brown, correspondence with the author, October 9, 2008.

5. Bill Buxton, correspondence with the author, October 17, 2008.

# Index

# About the Author

A best-selling author, **Roger Martin** is dean of the Rotman School of Management at the University of Toronto as well as a senior adviser to CEOs of large global companies. He is a columnist for *BusinessWeek* Online's Innovation and Design Channel and a regular contributor to the *Financial Times* Judgment Call column and to the *Washington Post* On Leadership blog. In 2007, *BusinessWeek* named him one of the ten most influential business professors in the world.